# CATHOLIC DOGMATICS

## FOR THE STUDY AND PRACTICE OF THEOLOGY

## VOLUME 1

### DOCTRINE OF CREATION

### ESCHATOLOGY

GERHARD LUDWIG MÜLLER

Translated By
WILLIAM HADFIELD-BURKARDT

*A Herder & Herder Book*
The Crossroad Publishing Company
New York

The Crossroad Publishing Company
www.crossroadpublishing.com

© 2012  9th edition Verlag Herder GmbH, Freiburg im Breisgau

Printed in the United States of America on acid-free paper.

The text of this book is set in 12/15 Adobe Garamond Pro.
Composition by Rachel Reiss.

**Library of Congress Cataloging-in-Publication Data**
available upon request.

Hardover: 978-0-8245-2232-2
Paperback: 978-0-8245-2233-9

# CONTENTS

# PREFACE TO THE AMERICAN EDITION OF DOGMATICS

The most important task in dogmatic theology is the mediation of God's free self-revelation in Jesus of Nazareth with the person's intellectual and ethical orientation in his world. The never-ending process of appropriating faith into human thought is characterized by the tension between the finality of God's self-communication in history and the repeatedly new attempts to translate them into the recipient's worldview and milieu.

*Katholische Dogmatik: Für Studium und Praxis der Theologie,* which was first published in 1994 in one volume, maintains a classic twelve-tract division, but puts them in an order that coordinates with a newly developed "outline of the structure of dogmatics" (vide p. xx) so that the first tracts to be treated have God's self-revelation as their subject (Series A) and then those tracts in which the person's response in faith are treated (Series B).

Since the single English edition is to appear in multiple volumes, this affords an opportunity to express the inner relationship of dogmatics as a whole, so that in each volume a tract from Series A is combined with the corresponding tract of Series B.

The present first volume includes the tracts on creation (protology) and last things (eschatology). They refer to the beginning and end points of God's historical action: He is the Creator of and the One who brings to fulfilment the human person and of all being.

Sincere thanks are due to the publisher Herder in Freiburg and New York for including this book in its publishing program.

Rome, in September, 2016
*Gerhard Cardinal Müller*
Prefect of the Congregation for the
Doctrine of the Faith

# INTRODUCTION

## 1. Goal and Program of the "Course Book Dogmatics"

Catholic Theology, as it is taught at universities, colleges and seminars, provides a sheer unlimited body of general and specialized knowledge. In the field of dogmatics in particular students are presented with such a massive amount of material that it is nearly impossible for them to get an *overview* of the subject, not to mention *insight* into the the heart of the matter. In light of the discrepancy between accumulated detailed knowledge and the absence of an intellectual synthesis, we might be reminded of the ironic words of Mephistopheles talking to the student in Goethe's Faust:

> Then he has the parts in his hand / What's missing—sadly!—is merely the spiritual thread.

Of course, the wide-ranging nature of Christian theology should not be simply trivialized as mere historical ballast. Its breadth is a necessary consequence of the universal claim to validity asserted by the Christian belief. The commitment to the truth that God has revealed himself in the creation, redemption and reconciliation as the beginning and the end of man and the world requires that theology as a principle does not exclude anything as a possible object of its reflections.

Throughout the 3500-year-old history of revelation, for all its isolated tensions and upheavals, a tradition of continuity in which Yahwe forms the subject of the revelation and in which the people of the covenant of the Old and New Testament finds its identity in the response of belief in the one Word of God proclaimed in history. Especially owing to the universality of the revelation manifested in Jesus Christ, the historical and eschatological understanding of truth in Christianity must be transmitted critically and positively with all the forms of human expression. Hence, it is crucial to confront the Christian self-conception with competing claims to the truth of concrete religions of men as well as with the theoretical and practical conceptions of the vision of man and the world in philosophy, history and the social and natural sciences.

Other tasks emcompassed by Catholic theology fall under the headings of the ecumenical movement and the inculturation in Latin American, Africa and Asia of a Christianity that was formed in Europe. Last but not least, it is integral to the study of theology that students familiarize themselves with the different auxiliary sciences (foreign languages, acquiring the philological and historical methods as part of a set of hermeneutical instruments).

The "spiritual thread" is the "thread of Ariadne," which leads out of the Labyrinth of theology's apparently inexhaustible material object. It is the consequence of comprehending the unity of theology in the source of the indivisible act of personal faith. The unity of theology depends on the antecedent unity of faith that in its profession and practice owes itself to the self-mediation of God. Inasmuch as theological reason is understood to mean the interpretation of faith, it proves itself to have been constituted along with belief. As belief itself, theology is determined by the event of man's encounter with the Word of God in the form of his self-mediation in the Christ event and the sending of the Spirit. Belief is the effect of the Holy Spirit.

> The general perspective that is needed, one that provides insight into the inner coherence of the individual themes and methods of theology, is the self-revelation of the triune God as mediated by the person and history of Jesus of Nazareth for the salvation of men.

Construction and structure of the Christian profession of faith (credo) reveal the three interlocking reference planes of theology. It is through belief that man's "I" or "we" is in a relation to God. This relation is mediated through Jesus Christ and remains present in the Church through the Holy Spirit. In this way, the three main mysteries of Christian belief are named: Trinity, incarnation, and the gift to men of the Spirit and of grace. To them are allocated the three main thematic groups: theology—Christology—anthropology. The individual tractates of the dogmatics can thus be presented in the context of this comprehensive perspective.

> The three basic dogmas of Christianity
> The Trinity of God:
> The persons of the one divine essence
> Incarnation:
> The incarnation of the eternal Son
> Spirit and grace:
> The coming of God in the Holy Spirit

Starting from the theology's task of setting the diversity of themes (material object) in relation to the unity of the perspective (formal object), the goals and the program for this "Course Book Dogmatics" are:

## 1. Basics

To the extent that material itself does not require a departure from this—it is outlined as follows:

I.      Current challenges of the subject matter
II.     The biblical foundations
III.    The historical development of dogma
IV.     The systematic representation

## 2. Guidance towards the Formation of Independent Theological Judgment.

In terms of genre, this course book is neither a theological encyclopedia nor does it take the place of a lexicon, nor is it an introduction to Christianity, much less a catechism. *It is a guide to dogmatic theology.*

## *2. Dogmatics as a Theological Discipline*

While the historical and practical subject areas of theology study the formal prerequisites of historical circumstances and the ethical, social and pastoral consequences of Christian faith, dogmatics considers the substance of the revelation in light of the central idea (formal object) of God's self-revelation as the origin and goal of the world, to the extent that this event makes a systematic (= speculative) understanding accessible. Formally, the dogmatics stems from the need of reason to convey the orientation towards God in the personal act of belief as the truth and life of man in a reasonable manner with the natural knowledge of worldly reality (Anselm of Canterbury, Proslogion 1: "Credo ut intelligam").

Dogmatics can be defined as follows:

> Dogmatics is the methodologically reflected presentation of the real substance and inner coherence of the "self-mediation of the threefold God in Jesus Christ as the salvation and life of man," as expressed through the medium of human language in the ecclesiastical profession of faith (= symbolum, dogma).

Though the name of this discipline (roughly since the eighteenth century) has been taken from the individual dogmas, dogmatics is not restricted to the dogmas in the formal sense: to certain doctrinal principles accepted in Catholic belief on divine authority due to a council or papal definition (e.g., the belief in Christ in the Nicene Creed or the dogma of the corporeal assumption of Mary in God's glory).

*Dogma* means here the whole of Christian belief in terms of the creed and practice of the Church.

## 3. The Structure of the Dogmatics

The purpose of dogmatics is to present the inner coherence of the revelation. However, this does not mean that God's revelation may be subordinated to human reason's absolute will to systematize (as this term is understood in German idealism). Human reason's manner of perception and historicity permit merely a *relative systematization* of the revelation that will always remain a mystery that eludes reason. In the context of unapproachable articles of faith (*articuli fidei*) only a summary representation in ordering perspectives and interrelated central ideas is possible. That is why a final system of the dogmatics has never asserted itself either.

In the neo-scholastic theology a structure crystallized in some 10-12 tractates that, however, has turned out in some instances to be somewhat schematic:

1. Theological epistemology;
2. Doctrine of the one and threefold God;
3. Creation doctrine;
4. Theological anthropology;
5. Christology/soteriology;
6. Mariology;
7. Ecclesiology;
8. Pneumatology;
9. Doctrine of grace;
10. Sacramental doctrine;
11. Eschatology.

By contrast, Karl Rahner suggests the abandonment of the tractates in thematic sequences (*Grundkurs des Glaubens*, Freiburg 1976
[Foundations of Christian Faith, Herder & Herder, 2005]). Each
of nine sequences is designed to provide access to a view of the
particular aspect and the Christian message as a whole: The Hearer
of the Message; Man in the Presence of Absolute Mystery; Threatened Radically by Guilt; The Event of God's Self-Communication;
The History of Salvation and Revelation; Jesus Christ; Christianity
as Church; Remarks on Christian Life; Eschatology.

This structure clearly reflects the necessity of a commitment
considering the questionable nature of man's existence that is conditioned in part by the anthropological-epistemological turning
point of the modern era.

In contrast to this, the "old dogmatics" starts directly with the theology of God. Following the profession of faith, attention is turned
to the unity and triunity of God: God as the foundation of his work
of salvation in creation, redemption and sanctification through to
consummation of man in the resurrection and in eternal life. Of
course, the anthropological dimension is also given consideration, to
the extent that it is included in the "I believe" or "We believe" with
which the *symbolum* begins (the God-likeness of man, the foundation of his spiritual creatureliness as *"desiderium naturale ad videndum Deum,"* personal character, ecclesiastical nature of belief, etc.).
However, the problem here consists in how the salvation historical
course of the revelation cannot be brought into congruence with the
structural point of departure of a systematization. In the event of
salvation history, God appears only at the end in the Christ Event as
the threefold God, who, however, of course, is already the threefold
God, author of the creation and the Old Testament salvation history.

As depicted in one volume of this course book (original edition
in German, Italian and Spanish translations), the now classic division of the tractates is retained but present in an inner coherence
that follows the event of the revelation and the condition of the
possibility of its acceptance in man.

Following the revelation-theological *Epistemology* as an introduction, *Series A* opens a more formal *Anthropology* in which the dependence of man on God is thematized. The *Doctrine of Creation* shows that the fundamental relatedness of man to God reflects God's free self-relation to his creature. The following three tractates show in terms of salvation history the self-revelation of the threefold God (*economic trinity*) as the subject of salvation history in the Old Testament and as the Father of Jesus Christ in the New Testament; the revelation of God in his Son (*Christology / Soteriology*) and in the Holy Spirit (*Pneumatology*). The salvation historical self-revelation of the threefold God then opens a view of God's threefold life (*doctrine of a trinitarian God*). This tractate is, so to speak, in the center of the whole theological thematic sequence.

The following section, *Series B*, is structured from the perspective of man's response in the history of faith corresponding to God's revelation treated in Series A. It opens with *Mariology*. In this section, in an exemplary manner, statements of the self-mediation of God related to anthropology make clear, inasmuch as Mary is the archetype of the blessed individual and of the Church as the congregation of the faith. Then, corresponding to God's self-revelation as Creator (protology), the theme of the consummation of man (*Eschatology*) follows, corresponding to the self-revelation of the Father, the community of the Church as God's people (*Ecclesiology*). Christology corresponds to the salvatory presence of Christ, the Head and Lord of the Church in the sacraments (*doctrine of the sacraments*), while subsequently—corresponding to the pneumatology—the *doctrine of grace* rounds off the dogmatic discourse.

The structure can be illustrated by the following "outline."

In the edition of the course book in several volumes, as it is presented here, each tractate in Series A is linked with its corresponding tractate in Series B.

The first volume contains the tractates on the creation doctrine and eschatology.

## 4. Outline of the Structure of the Dogmatics

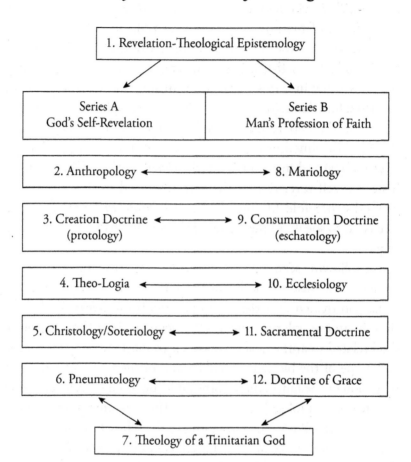

# GOD'S SELF-REVELATION AS THE CREATOR OF THE WORLD

*(The Doctrine of Creation)*

# I.

# THEMES AND PERSPECTIVES OF A THEOLOGY OF THE CREATION

## 1. Creation—A Theological Concept

The Nicene Constantinopolitan Creed begins with the fundamental statement: "I believe in one God, the Father almighty, creator of heaven and earth, of all things visible and invisible." (DH 150)

As can be seen from the structure of the sentence, the substance of this belief is not a statement about the world; it states a faith in God as a personal reality (*credere in Deum*). This is also an expression of faith in him (*credere Deo*), which is impossible without the belief in his existence and his active sovereignty (*credere Deum*). In the light of this personal faith in God, man can designate the world, in a universal qualification, as creation. Hence, the doctrine of creation proves to be a transcendental perspective on the world at the level of a personal relationship to God. Due to the Christian understanding of God as a spiritual, free, omniscient and omnipotent personal reality, Christian belief in creation differs in principle from mythical cosmogonies and theogonies, natural philosophic and natural scientific doctrines of how the world originated, but also from the natural theology of metaphysics.

The personal faith-based relationship to God the Creator is rooted in Israel's historical experience of God. This is why the *Symbolum* identifies the "Father almighty," specifically the God of the Covenant, as the universal Creator of the world. The God who liberated Israel from slavery, the God of the Covenant, the law and the messianic promise, is identical with the Sovereign Creator, Ruler and Consummator of "heaven and earth" (Gen 1:1), the God and Father of all men and peoples. The God of the creation and the Covenant is also identical with the Consummator of the world in the "creation of the new heaven and the new earth" (Isa 65:17), when he brings together Israel with all the peoples for the "revelation of his glory" (Isa 66:19) in the eschatological communion of saints.

The belief in God the Creator does not flow from two completely different sources. Belief in God the Creator and Redeemer is rooted in the one experience of his power in history, in the cosmos and in the life of the individual man. In terms of this fundamental experience of God's powerful presence, the horizon extends to the all-encompassing origin (protology) and the entire and final perfection of the world (eschatology). God reveals himself in the present from the core of the personal experience of God as the transcendent origin and transcendent goal of man and the world. The conceptual rendering of the belief in creation is a contribution to the general historical development of the understanding of God in salvation history. Only in the light of the Christ event does God the Creator reveal his identity as God and as the Father of Jesus Christ.

The belief in creation takes on further aspects: the eternal Word or the eternal Son as the mediator of creation, the trinitarian God as the origin and purpose, the eschatological perfection of the world in light of Christ, the Son of God, and the Holy Spirit.

> Hence, "creation" designates the universally transcendental relationship between the world and God which shines in the spiritual and free relationship between man and the world and history as both their underlying foundation and consummating goal.

## 2. Creation: God's Original Self-Revelation

One essential principle of any human speech about God stands out here: God is known through the historical world and its human community, he mediates himself indirectly as its absolute Author through the world's existence, its guidance and perfection as expressed in the totality of its existence and working. "Since the beginning of the world", i.e. coextensively with the existence of the created reality, God reveals his "invisible reality", his "eternal power and divinity" (Rom 1:19 f.), by making himself knowable through the light (*intellectus agens*) of human reason (*intellectus possibilis*).

The created world is not an exchangeable medium that God takes up casually for the purpose of revealing himself. The being of the world which lights up man's acquisition of knowledge is how God irrefutably penetrates human reason. Wherever man in his transcendental self-awareness enquires into existential meaning and human purpose, he encounters God at least tangentially and implicitly as the transcendent foundation of finite existence and knowledge. Because in man's experience of himself and the world, God, the free origin of both world and man, of finite existence and finite knowledge, proclaims himself as the divine mystery, the discussion must be explicitly about God's self-revelation. This original knowledge of God as the Creator also goes far beyond any philosophical approach to God as the transcendent first cause of the world, because this original experience of the divine is itself already a salvation-mediating encounter with God.

The Christian concept of creation brings man and the world into a special co-ordinate system in relation to God's personal transcendence, consequently, to God's personal immanence in the specific history of his self-mediation in the Word and in the Mediator of the Covenant, Jesus Christ:

- God himself is in terms of his essence and being infinitely dissimilar from the world. He possesses himself such that

his possession of self and disposition of his personal reality
is unlimited.

- Man as a creature is a being of this world and at the same
time is the addressee of God's self-revelation as the Creator
and Partner in the history of the Covenant.

- The world as the creation is not a part of God or a moment
in an intra-divine dialectical process; the world as the creation is the environment of man and a medium of the revelation of the glory and power of God.

- Hence, the theological concept of creation consists of three
interwoven reference levels:

  1) *The act of creation*: The creation, as an act of God, coincides with the God's act of being existential act itself
  through which he autonomously calls into existence the
  totality of all non-divine existence and lets all individual
  beings really subsist individually in the specificity of
  their nature. What is created is essentially distinct from
  God, but from the divine act establishing reality, God is
  intimately and deeply present in all creatures in a manner which corresponds to their finite natures. This basic
  creative relationship to the world unfolds into individual
  aspects which designate the beginning, the execution and
  the perfection of the created things of this world. God
  the Creator is from the beginning (*creatio ex nihilo*) the
  unceasing foundation which preserves all things in their
  existence and form (*conservatio mundi*). He steers and
  effects the world's progress for the salvation of creatures
  through his care and providence (*providentia Dei*). Man
  is not guided to his ultimate goal from without but rather
  by means of and within human freedom as the correspondence of divine and human freedom (*concursus divinus*).

  2) *The created world*: Creation also means the totality of all
  things created: "the heavens and earth" (cf. Gen 1:1; the
  universe, the realm of space, the cosmos or "the world").
  Of course, creation is more than merely the sum of what

exists. The creation is God's medium of self-revelation and self-communication. This is why God's creative activity culminates in the one creature which, thanks to its intellectual endowment, is capable of self-transcendence. God's creative activity is centered on man because man can transcend the creatureliness of the world and, in the light of his self-knowledge as a creature, can rise to become the personal interlocutor of God's Word. The creation has its inner ultimate purpose in the Covenant of Grace.

3) *The order of creation:* Both in its existence and in its essence, the order of creation is an indication of God's goodness, sovereignty and wisdom, reflected in the functional structure of matter and in the processuality which preserves and bears life. God reveals his salvific will in the order of the world.

The order of creation includes the enablement of man to bear responsibility actively for:

- Material nature (ecology, environmental ethics);
- Human environment: the political, social and economic management of the habitat (moral theology, social ethics) derived from the reality of creation;
- Personhood: man's realization of the quest for meaning, and man's transcendental reliance on God as the hearer of God's Word and, consequently, religion, faith, community of the Church (philosophy of the revelation).

## 3. Important Doctrinal Statements on the Creation Doctrine

1. The Synod of Constantinople 543 condemned the doctrine of the "Origenists," that God's power is finite, and he created all that he could comprehend and think (DH 410).

2.  Regarding the "Priscillianists" (a Manichaean–Gnostic sect), canons 5–13 of the First Synod of Braga (561) invoke an anathema against all those who defend the following views:

    (can. 5): Human souls or angels come from the substance of God (DH 455),

    (can. 7): The devil was not first a good angel; he had no Creator but is himself the principle and substance of evil (DH 457);

    (can. 8): The devil made some of the creatures in the world, and he damages by his own power the world and man (e.g., by storms; DH 458);

    (can. 9): Human souls and bodies are by their fate bound to the stars (DH 459);

    (can. 11): Condemnation of human marriage and loathing of the procreation of children (DH 461);

    (can. 12): The formation of the human body is the work of the devil, and there is no such thing as the resurrection of the flesh (DH 462);

    (can. 13): The creation of all flesh is not the work of God but of bad angels (DH 463).

3.  Against the idealistic, Neoplatonic understanding of the creation and the idea of a natural cycle, the Lateran Synod (649) emphasizes the realistic salvation historic orientation of Church doctrine: can. 1: *Deus Trinitas est creatrix* (Creator) *omnium et protectrix* (protector): DH 501.

4.  In 1208 Pope Innocent III prescribed to the Waldensians (who, like the Albigensians, Catharists and Lombards, taught that matter was evil and that the devil created it from nothing) this profession of faith: The one and threefold God is the creator of all things, corporeal and spiritual, he is the one author of the OT and NT; and is the Creator of all things from nothing (DH 790).

5.  The *caput Firmiter* of the Lateranense IV (1215) completely rejects Catharism: "We firmly believe and confess without reservation that there is only one true God, eternal, infinite, and unchangeable, incomprehensible, almighty, and ineffable, the Father, the Son and the Holy Spirit... < They are > *the one principle of the universe*, the *Creator of all things, visible and invisible*, spiritual and corporeal, who by his almighty power *from the beginning of time* made at once *out of nothing* both orders of creatures, the spiritual and the corporeal, that is, the angelic and the earthly, and then the human creature, who, as it were, shares in both orders, being composed of spirit and body. For the devil and the other demons were indeed created by God naturally good, but they became evil by their own doing. As for man, he sinned at the suggestion of the devil" (DH 800).

6.  Pope John XXII criticized (1329) some articles written by Meister Eckhart (whereby what Meister Eckhart meant by these teachings is a matter of dispute). The following teachings are refuted: the eternal co-existence of the world with God; the complete parallelism of the eternal begetting of the Son from the Father with the creation; all creatures are one pure nothing; there is something in the soul that is uncreated and incapable of being created (DH 951–53, 976f.).

7.  Against Manichaean dualism the Church taught at the Council of Florence (1442) in the Decree for the Jacobites in the Bull of Union *Cantate Domino*: "The one true God, Father, Son, and Holy Spirit, is the Creator of all things, visible and invisible, who when he so *willed*, out of his *bounty*, made all creatures, spiritual as well as corporeal. They are good since they were made by him who is the highest good, but they are mutable because they were made out of nothing. . . . There is no such thing as a nature of evil, because all nature, as nature, is good. . . . One and

the same God is the author of the OT and the NT." There
are not "two first principles, one of the visible things, the
other of invisible things" (DH 1333–36).

8. In response to the Catholic theologians G. Hermes und
   A. Günther, whose orientation had been too influenced
   by Kant and Hegel, the Synode der Rheinischen Kirchen-
   provinz in Köln (1860) takes a position against pantheism,
   deism and the Hegelian understanding of a "becoming
   God." Set forth in detail: God is complete in himself. He
   is immutable. His becoming is not dependent on the becoming of the world. God creates the world, free of any
   inner compulsion or outer force, in order to convey to
   it his goodness. God could have created another world.
   The world was created by God in time. The purposes of
   the creation are the happiness of man and the revelation
   of the glory of God as well as his perfections, especially
   his wisdom, power and goodness. A distinction is drawn
   between *gloria Dei subiectiva* (= prayer, gratitude, the
   worship of God by man) and *gloria Dei obiectiva* (= God
   stands revealed in his works), while, in turn, regarding
   the gloria Dei obiectiva, a distinction is drawn between
   the gloria Dei *interna* and the gloria Dei *externa* (NR
   303–313).

9. The Vaticanum I had the same errors in mind when in the
   constitution *Dei Filius* (chap. 1, can. 1–5) it teaches:
   chap. 1: God is a singular, completely simple and immu-
      table spiritual being. He is really and essentially dis-
      tinct from the world (re et essentia a mundo distinctus).
      The definition from the Lateranse IV is repeated as the
      definition of creation.
   Specifically can. 3: "If anyone says that the substance and
      essence of God and all things is one and the same: let
      him be anathema."

Can. 4: "If anyone says that finite beings, the corporeal as well as the spiritual...have emanated from the divine substance, or that the divine essence becomes all things by self-manifestation or self-evolution, or lastly that God is the universal or indefinite being which, by self-determination, constitutes the universality of beings, differentiated in genera, species, and individuals: let him be anathema." (Hence, the being of beings is not God.)

Can. 5: "If anyone refuses to confess that the world and all things contained in it, the spiritual as well as the material, were in their whole substance produced by God out of nothing; or says that God created, not by an act of will free from all necessity, but with the same necessity by which he necessarily loves himself; or denies that the world was made for the glory of God: let him be anathema." (DH 3001–03; 3021–25)

10. Finally, the Vaticanum II addressed questions of the creation doctrine, especially in the Pastoral Constitution *Gaudium et spes* (1965): Man has received from God the ability and the mission to manage the world in a responsible manner, to foster community in the family and in society. In his cultural and scientific achievements man is not God's rival. The Christian message of eternal life does not distract man from taking *responsibility for the world* and providing the *care needed for a human world*, it challenges him to accept explicitly this responsibility and provide this care (GS 33–39).

## 4. The Dogma of Creation in Its Constitutive Elements

The term creation (as an act) is understood to mean the production of a thing in its entire substance, nothing being presupposed either uncreated or created (cf. Thomas, S. th. I q. 65 a. 3: "creatio est productio alicuius rei secundum suam totam substantiam nullo praesupposito quod sit vel increatum vel ab aliquo creatum").

The dogma of creation contains both theological statements in the narrow sense (i.e., statements about God) as well as cosmological statements (about the world as it is) and anthropological statements (about man).

## Statements about God:

- The threefold God is the origin and ultimate purpose of the whole of creation and salvation history (DH 171; 790; 800; 1333). Father, Son and Holy Spirit are not three origins, but the *one* origin of the whole creation (DH 501; 1331).
- God reveals himself in and towards the world in his transcendent person–reality. In contrast with pantheistic, emanationist process-philosophical ideas according to which God is naturally caught up in the world process and in the constitution or perfection of his essence in proceeding through the world realizes himself, the First Vatican Council emphasizes the absolute transcendence and freedom, the subjectivity and the person–reality of God (DH 3001).
- God's aseity (*aseitas*), which holds him aloof of natural involvement in the world process (God's immutability), as God's personal transcendence, is simultaneously also the reason for his personal immanence in the world, his forcefulness in history and his spontaneous influence. This is directed against a deistic idea according to which God only has an influence on the origin of the world, but not the course of history (D 2902; 3003).
- The presence and immanence of God in the world is given by the Person of the Father, the "Maker of heaven and earth," the Person of the Son, "by whom all things were made" and the Person of the Holy Spirit, who is the "Lord and giver of life." The self-revelation of the threefold God is finally completed

when the Son in the Holy Spirit turns over his kingdom to the Father, "so that God may be all in all" (1 Cor 15:28).

## Statements about the world:

- Everything that exists apart from God exists due to God's creative activity. Creatures are not divine appearances. The world possesses in the form of individual things and living beings a created subsistence which lends individuals in the scope of their nature their own reality, activity and value.
- God creates the world by sovereignly positing finite being (in existence and form) without resorting to any pre-existing matter (against the idea that God is a mere demiurge). Only God can create out of nothing (DH 800).
- God creates, along with the world, space and time as perceptible forms accessible to man, in which he can order the manifold empirical existence of sensual experience. The mere thought–object of time eternal and an endless expanse of empty space without matter has nothing to do with the eternity which is identical with God's essence.
- The created world is from its origin *one* (in opposition to metaphysical dualism). But it consists, at least in man, of the duality of the principles of spirit and matter, which differ essentially from one another, with the spirit–soul as the unifying principle (in opposition to metaphysical monism).
- God creates the world *in freedom*, without any need for an inner necessity or outer force. As God's freedom is identical with his essence, in relation to his creation it signifies the rendering possible of a certain contribution to the freedom created in the divine realization of freedom. God's freedom vis à vis the world has its anthropological reflection in the enabling of human freedom for self-realization in love and for the participation in the life of the threefold God.
- The *"motive" for the act of creation* is God's essence itself, his *love* (GS 19) and his *goodness* (DH 3002): "Not for the

increase of his own happiness or for the acquirement of his perfection, but in order to manifest his perfection through the benefits that he bestows on creatures."

- The motive of the creation has its correspondence in the world to the extent that all created things and living beings by reason of their nature and in their nature (i.e. in the mode of participation in being which realizes them) *are* themselves *good* (cf. Gen 1:31: "God looked at everything he had made, and found it very good"). The inner goodness of the creature also includes the materiality of the world and the corporeality of man.
- For this reason, against Manichaeism, it can be deduced from creation theology that moral *evil* has *no created nature* (DH 1333). From the perspective of creation theology, tracing moral evil back to created nature or stating that creation's finiteness is accompanied quasi inevitably by misfortune and evil in no way takes wickedness seriously but rather, on the contrary, treats misfortune as trivial and provides moral evil with a specious excuse. Moral evil has no intrinsic existence. It coexists with a personally created will which, against its own salvation, turns against the order of the world and the orientation towards God and, in so doing, exposes itself in its abysmal perversity (*mysterium iniquitatis*).
- The superordinate *purpose of creation* is the revelation of the glory of God (DH 3025). Corresponding to this is the revelation of the ultimate purpose of man: participating in God's life, attaining to beatitude.
- In revealing himself as the beginning, the middle and the ultimate goal of all of creation, God preserves man's world and guides the history of mankind (GS 39).

## Statements about man:

- Man is the goal of the act of creation and the inner movement of the world process. Man is created in the image of

God as a spiritual and physical *essentia*. Through his personhood, he is free to act in relation to the world. An integral aspect of his being is his personal and transcendental relationship with God.

- The sovereignty of the human spirit, its cultural formation and productivity do not characterize man as a rival to the Creator but are ". . . a sign of God's grace and the flowering of his own mysterious design."
- For man, created in God's image, is called upon

> to govern the world with justice and holiness: a mandate to relate himself and the totality of things to Him Who was to be acknowledged as the Lord and Creator of all. Thus, by the subjection of all things to man, the name of God would be wonderful in all the earth. (GS 34)

# 5. The Creation Theology within the Structure of Church Dogmatics

## a) Structural Problems in Creation Theology

Creation theology does not stand at the beginning as an isolated tractate. Its purpose is not to describe a static and ahistorical relationship between God and the world in juxtaposition to a salvation historical experience of God. The creation is in itself the prehistory of the relationship between God and man. And the theological dimension of worldly reality constituted by the act of creation cannot be circumvented by the sin of man. Creation signifies God's first self-revelation to man through the creation of the world, to the extent that God calls man into existence in the unity of nature and grace. In this context, "nature" means the creaturely substance through which man is radically dissimilar from God in the Creator–creature–difference, yet his humanness

is energized to accept his self freely due the vouchsafed nearness
to God. It was sin which restricted the fulfillment of human
creatureliness. But sin cannot cancel God's self-revelation in the
creation as the final salvation of man. The commitment of God
the Creator's salvific will in the face of sin thus means the beginning of a salvation history whose objective is redemption and
the adoption by means of the granted contribution to the filial
behavior of the Logos made man in relation to the Father in the
presence of the Holy Spirit.

At the beginning of Catholic dogmatics, the doctrine of creation offers a complete overview of the structure of theology. The
creation doctrine must provide an explanation of the basic understanding of reality of the theology, its conception of history
and its idea of the world and man. It is in creation theology
where the Christian understanding of God is developed in the
form of basic statements that, first, relate to the question of how
God reveals himself as a Creator and as the Consummator of
man through the reality of creation in man's reasoned understanding of himself and, second, to how man must understand
himself in the analysis of its basic existential experiences as a
theological essence.

The subject of creation theology is God, who reveals himself in
the worldly reality of man as the beginning and the end (*De Deo
creatore qua principium et finis omnis creaturae*).

## b) The Tension between the Views of Salvation History and Systematic Theology

"Creation" as a fundamental theological statement grew out of
humanity's historical experience of God. It can only be formu-
lated in theological depth as a result of the Christ event and the
sending of the Holy Spirit. However, the theology of a trinitarian
God and a developed creation theology factually anticipates the
process of acquiring knowledge. Hence, there is a certain degree

of counteraction between the order of being and the order of knowledge.

## c) The Particularity of Christianity and Its Claim to Universality

The Christian faith is built on Israel's historically contingent experience of faith and on the contingency of the historical person Jesus. It is from this underivable nature of the particular that the vision expands to include humanity in general as reflected in the history of religion, world history, and the history of ideas.

The claim to universality led theologians as early as the apologists of the second century to search for common denominators, based on how they fundamentally experienced man, the world and the divine, that would make the God of the Israelites and the Father of Jesus Christ, the universal Creator and the Consummator of man, accessible to the "pagans." This is how a bridge was built to the religious experience of mankind, to the reflection of an understanding of God in the natural theology of the philosophers, especially of Plato and Aristotle. This approach also encompasses the disagreement with the natural science perception of empirical conditions, the origin of the world, and the hominization of man based on a process of biological evolution. This encounter is certainly not one-sided. With the help of philosophical categories and the scientific insights of cosmology, theology is capable of formulating the creation doctrine more precisely, of setting aside misunderstandings and of communicating with the worldview of modern man and with an understanding of reality developed by philosophical reason.

However, there is a certain degree of risk involved to the extent that, in the course of the history of theology, the doctrine of creation was threatened with naturalization. Creation can be easily misunderstood as a salvifically neutral rough construction if God is only introduced in a general way as the Creator of the world (as in deism or in a monotheistic cosmology), instead of understanding that the creation from the outset is the beginning of a salvifically relevant self-revelation of the personal reality of God–Creator.

## d) The Inner Correlation of the Creation and Redemption Order

It is through the original sin that the original unity of God's self-revelation as the *Creator* of man as well as *Consummator* has become blurred to mankind. The dualistic Manichaeistic gnosis magnifies this experience of difference to such an extent that it posits the scission within God himself. An evil god of creation in the Old Testament stands diametrically opposed to the good god of redemption in the New Covenant. By contrast, Christian theology has always emphasized the unity of God, who revealed himself as the Creator and, in light of sin, as man's Redeemer.

Because, since Augustine, Western theology treated the relationship to God largely in the polarity of grace and sin (as did later reformation theology with its concentration on the problematic of justification), a neglect of the creation theology was always a looming danger. It was overlooked that God's self-revelation in the act of creation embraces all the historically variable realizations of the human relationship to God in belief or disbelief and that the reality of creation always stands ahead of the parentheses within which a theology of the original sin and the grace of redemption is developed.

As far back as the church fathers (Irenaeus of Lyons) and especially since scholasticism's reading of Aristotle (Thomas Aquinas), Catholic theology has attached importance to a depiction of the unity of the creation and redemption teachings which has its origin in the unity of God. The dialectic of sin and grace must be encompassed by an existential–ontological experience of the creatureliness of man and, hence, an experience of his dependence on a sacred mystery that is revealed as God and, in the history of Israel, pronounces itself to be the God–Redeemer of all men.

# 6. *The Creation Theology in Distinction to Religious and Scientific Doctrines of the Origin of the World*

The existence of Humanity's rich treasure of doctrines of how the world originated from religious mythology, natural philosophy and natural science shows that the question of the origin of the world and the status of man represents an anthropological constant. The mere existence of the world and its order suggests a dependence on a higher power, whether this takes the form of gods, a supreme spirit, a divine numinosum or the principle of a creative dynamic force of "nature."

All these concepts differ from each other in terms of content, approach and objective from the Judeo-Christian (and, in their dependence, also from the Islamic) understanding of the world as creation because here "God" means a personal, sovereign and independent power who, in his existence and form, is free in relation to the world.

## a) Mythical World Doctrines of the Origin of the World

Of greater significance for the literary form and the worldview background of the Old Testament hymns of creation and prehistoric human history (Gen 1–11) are the world origin myths from ancient Mesopotamian cultures: The Sumerian poem *Eridu Genesis* (2000 BC), the Sumerian Epic of *Gilgamesh* (650 BC), the Babylonian epic *Enûma Eliš* (twelfth and eleventh centuries BC) and from Egypt, the *Hymn to the Sun* by the Egyptian King Akhenaten (1360 BC) as well as the *Hymn to Amun* at the time of Ramses II.

The direction of at least a political monotheism is reflected in the Memphite Theology on the Shabaka Stone (roughly 700 BC). Ptah, the ruling god of Memphis, appears as the general author and "creator" of the Ennead and man. He brought forth the world spiritually through his divine words. These come from his heart and are the essence of things.

Already what is known as the *Instruction to Merikare* (Egypt roughly 2200–2040 BC) ascribes to a (possibly monotheistically understandable) god the creation, preservation and juridical order of the world. Striking are the literary similarities with the Yahwistic hymn of creation (Gen 2):

> Well tended is mankind—the cattle of the god. He made sky and earth for their sake, he subdued the water monster, he made breath for their noses to live. They are his images, who came from his body...

(Wim van den Dungen, *The Royal Instruction of Khety to Merikare*; cf. M. Eliade, *Geschichte der religiösen Ideen*. Quellentexte, Fr 1981, 90; this also contains a collection of world origin poems from various mythical religions).

Beyond the immediate environment of the biblical world attention must also be paid to doctrines of the origin of the world and gods (cosmogonies and theogonies) of Greek mythology (Homer, Hesiod) as well as the Asian Vedas (Upanishads; Bhagavad Gita) and the various myths of the African and Native American religions.

They all remain committed to a polytheistic image of God. God and man are encompassed in the divine cosmos and subordinated to the universal rhythm of becoming and dissolution of life (cf. vegetation and fertility cults). A cosmocentric understanding of the world is linked to a divinization and sacralization of world/nature.

In the religious studies (cf. F. Heiler, *Erscheinungsformen und Wesen der Religion*, St 21979, 471–474) four types have been identified:

1. The spontaneous origin of the world, for example from the "world egg";
2. The origin of the world through the sexual coupling of the gods or the self-impregnation of a hermaphroditic divinity;
3. The processing of matter or the taming of the powers of chaos and their formation into a cosmos, whereby human

beings were able to proceed from the deified things, such as an animal, a tree or the tears of the gods;

4. The creation from "nothing" (no existing matter; not meant in a philosophical sense) by magical primordial words or spells uttered by the gods.

Alongside these, there are also religions or philosophical world-views that do not refer to any origin of the world and whose final horizon is assumed to be an eternal cycle (for example, Buddhism).

Mythological are also the dualistic world origin theories. They say that the world is where the struggle between good and evil play out which can be traced back to the creation of good or evil gods (Iranian Zoroastrianism, the gnosis, Manichaeism), theories that were also highly influential in the Greco-Roman world of the Roman Empire.

## b) Philosophical Cosmologies

Among the Ionic natural philosophers (starting from the sixth century) mythologies lose their captivating power. The substance of the myths and their claim to truth must be tested as reasonable explanations of the world's reality. The pre-Socratics address the major philosophic questions of being, becoming and dissolution, the one and the many, as well as the original ground of all appearances. The first principle of the world, the arché (ἀρχή), from which everything comes to be, is the ground continuously present in all things, their nature (φύσις) (elemental stuffs: fire, earth, water or air; the apeiron (ἄπειρον), the everliving fire for Heraclitus and, later, the stoics; or, for the Pythagoreans, the number). The world process is generated by the various conditions of the elemental stuffs and their order within the totality. What appears is a fluctuation between the unity at the origin and the multitude of appearances.

In response to the question whether spiritual principles can be identified above and beyond material principles, the pre-Socratic Anaxagoras arrives at the idea of a world mind separate from the things of the world. This mind, by means of its knowledge and thought, is the cause of the changing mixture and separation of the material masses.

In contrast to this, the atomists Leucippus and Democritus (and, later, the Epicureans) rule out spiritual or divine causes. There are only material causes. Only these have being. Beyond them is nothing but the void. The changing conditions of the world, as they appear to us, are caused by mechanical forces. Through them the indivisible existential (the atoms) enter in each case into another, complex relationship with each other, depending position, form and expansion. This mechanical-atomistic materialism necessarily leads to "atheism." Recourse to a divine principle is superfluous to explain the world.

### c) The Natural Theology of Philosophy

In response to monism and materialism, Plato, Aristotle and, later, Plotinus as well, maintained the reality of the spirit and, hence, also a transcendent-divine principle of the world. Instead of the atomistic teaching of the limitless number of possible worlds, i.e., the illimitable variety of constellations of atoms, they teach the uniqueness of this world and correspondingly also the uniqueness of its absolute foundation, specifically, God. Their philosophic monotheism, however, does not at all correspond to the Bible's understanding of God in his absolute autonomy and historical power. Here, the relationship between God and the world is not at all conveyed by this concept of creation. God merely appears as the world's builder (Plato) or as the first unmoved mover of the world's movement in its new interaction of spiritual forms and matter in continuous transition of actuality and potentiality (Aristotle).

According to the neo-Platonic concept of Plotinus (AD 205–270) in the *Enneads*, the world is created emanatively through the radiation from the perfectly simple superessential One in the same multitude of stages and limitations as they present themselves to us in the variety of earthly appearances (ideas, souls, matter). Specifically, the world is formed by the world spirit within the frame of reference of the eternal ideas. The road leads by necessity from plurality back to the primordial unity. So the world is marked by a double movement of the emergence from the one and return to it (*exitus-reditus* scheme).

The historical influence of Plato, Aristotle and Plotinus is highly significant for the rational communication of the Christian belief in God and his creation. However, a substantial transformation and further development of their basic ideas is necessary to be able to come to be helpful in rational theological discourse.

In Plato's writings there is no idea of a world origin in time. They treat a fundamental dependence of the sensually perceptible and mutable world on the eternal, immutable, abstract ideas and, most importantly, on the highest idea of the good. The sensual world is fashioned by the demiurge based on the eternal ideas. But all created substance proceed from one cause. This world of appearance is created by a lesser or greater participation in the eternal world of ideas.

In the dialog which is important for this theme, *Timaeus* 29a–29b, contains the words:

> If the world be indeed fair and the artificer good, it is manifest that he must have looked to that which is eternal... for the world is the fairest of creations and he is the best of causes. And having been created in this way, the world has been framed in the likeness of that which is apprehended by reason and mind and is unchangeable, and must therefore of necessity, if this is admitted, be a copy of something. Now it is all-important that the beginning of everything should be according to nature.

Hence, the sensible world of appearance is a movable copy of eternity. Plato states the motive (ibid. 29e):

> Let me tell you then why the creator made this world of generation. He was good, and the good can never have jealousy of anything... And being free from jealousy, he desired that all things should be as like himself as they

could be. Wherefore he set in order the visible world, which he found in disorder. . . .

In the twelfth book of his *Metaphysics* Aristotle criticizes Plato's theory of ideas because it only allows for the concrete world of experience to be an image of a primordial world of ideas, thus underestimating the former's own reality. By contrast, Aristotle proceeds from concrete material being and considers it in its beingness. The identity of each being is determined by its form (its quiddity; *substantia secunda*). Each of these forms is realized in matter. Hence, changes, movements and becoming of the individual are nothing other than a finding or losing of the substantial form.

In the individual thing, form and matter are directly associated to the extent that the generality of the form is individualized by matter. The matter turns a general form into an individual being subsisting in itself. Each individual existence is determined by the two immanent causes of form and matter. Beyond this, to be able to explain becoming and dissolution, two further causes are necessary: the efficient cause and the final cause. This can explain how various forms act on each other.

Since, on a higher level of abstraction, form and matter relate to each other in a manner similar to potentiality and actuality, i.e., as a possibility and its fulfillment in reality, one can only explain movement as the continuous transition of potentiality to actuality if one can refer to an already existent reality, an act or a form. This leads to the metaphysical concept causality: "*Omne ens quod movetur ab alio movetur*—everything that is moved is moved by something else." However, in the sequence of movements, one must return to a first reality, a first action or a purely spiritual form. This first efficient cause of all movement can itself not be a composition of potentiality and reality because, otherwise, it would need another efficient cause which would set in motion the formative force of its actuality in reference to matter.

Aristotle thus arrives at a definition of the essence of the prime mover. He is absolutely simple and unique. He is the most truly real existence, pure act, spiritual form free of any matter. He is pure thought of himself or absolute transcendence. In himself he is life, beatitude and pure thought and not subject to changeableness and determinability as are worldly things. In this philosophical monotheism of Aristotle, however, God is by no means understood in the Christian sense of a Creator. Here, God appears more as a final limiting concept of human thought. He does not appear in relation to it as a free subject who can "predicate" his own freedom through his Word and his historical acts, i.e., can make his freedom knowable through his Word and historical acts; instead, he always remains a kind of predicate in connection with the world.

In this instance God, as a purely spiritual form, is merely the prime mover that moves existing forms to enter into a marriage with pure, still completely indeterminate prime matter, i.e., the purest potential (far from all materiality) (*materia prima*). According to Aristotle the forms and the materia prima have always existed. In the worldly process, only individuals perish. The essences are eternal. There is also no coincidental origin of species because pure forms have indeed always existed. The essences and species in their individual compositions with the materia prima are the foundation of becoming. But they are never their product. The purpose and goal of becoming merge with the form. So Aristotle is not only thinking causally but rather also teleologically in a manner which appears impossible to a mechanistic view of the world.

With the emergence of modern natural science in the fifteenth and sixteenth centuries, the tensions surrounding the Christian creation theology arose in particular because this was expressed and presented in the categories of Aristotelian hylemorphism, transcendent causality and teleology.

### d) The Worldview of Modern Science

The conflicts between the Judeo-Christian belief and modern natural sciences largely revolve around questions related to the doctrine of creation. Since theology, a transcendental science, treats the personal relationship between God and man, and natural science, which examines the structure of matter, are fundamentally different in terms of their respective object and method, there should be no reason for friction between the two. The historical conflicts are triggered mainly by questions of cosmology, more precisely, to the inquiry into the conditions of the origin of the cosmic world and the origin of man.

If the literary genre of the biblical creation narratives had been properly interpreted from the outset, it would have been clear that the ways in which the narratives are presented, influenced as they are by worldviews, are not themselves among the objects of belief (DV 12). Because for the relationship between God and man, the question of a heliocentric or geocentric worldview is without import (Galileo dispute), no less than the material continuity of man with the evolution of living things (Charles Darwin's theory of descent, cf. GS 36). But it is not these conflicts which take place on a more superficial level which were decisive but rather the fundamental philosophical conception of reality underlying theological thought, on the one hand, and natural-scientific thought on the other.

Against the background of certain transformations in medieval and early modern philosophy (nominalism), the Aristotelian teaching of the four causes had become questionable. The empirical and experimental research of the natural sciences no longer understood matter as a metaphysical cause. Instead, they reduced matter to the aspect of quantity (mass and energy) and homogeneous distribution of its parts in space and described their relation to each other by applying the rules of mathematical logic. Out of the "mechanistic" worldview which emerged from this there crystalized an image of God as the prime mover of the world machine in which the functionality of all the parts with each other proves to be the revelation of the superior intelligence of its designer (the image of God preferred by deism and physico-theology).

This image of God had to be problematic, when it could be explained that the hypothesis of a world designer was no longer necessary. God's redundancy as a working hypothesis of the natural sciences was also apparent specifically in the knowledge of the hominization process. If the creation can no longer be understood with the aid of a theory stating that species have been constant from the beginning (Carl von Linné) but, instead, the development of species is shown to be determined by external influences on a dynamic living process (selection, selective breeding, genetic mutation), then there is no need for an intervention from outside to explain the origin of man. Moreover, in a development determined by coincidence and an external constellation of conditions a teleology can no longer be proven. God is eliminated as a *causa efficiens transcendentalis et causa finalis*. Various scientists interpret the Darwinian theory of universal evolution of all living creations and a theory of the self-organization of matter (Jacques Monod and Manfred Eigen), which exclude a supranatural intervention of a higher being, as a disproof of creation theology and as a basis for atheism (F. Wuketits, *Evolutionstheorien*, Da 1988, 29).

But all conceptions which assume either God's necessity or redundancy as a working hypothesis in the natural sciences for the physical cosmology or biology, remain stuck to the physico-theological image of God and fail to consider the basic difference between the empirical-mathematical description of matter and the broader philosophical enquiry into the meaning of existence in the first place or the difference between existence and nothingness. Theology can only be transmitted by means of a general philosophical enquiry into reality with the results of modern natural science. The dialog becomes problematic when the findings of the natural sciences are used to support a materialistic philosophy.

Today, the two opposing theories of natural science, one which sees the beginning of the world in time (called "the big-bang theory") or in its timelessness and spatial unlimitlessness (St. Hawking, *A Brief History of Time: From the Big Bang to Black Holes*, 1988), move on another level than the philosophical enquiry into existence and the theological enquiry into God. They are thus neither a natural scientific confirmation or disproof of the belief in God the Creator.

According to the observation of an expanding universe (cf. the theory of the American astronomer Edwin Hubble of the radial recession movement of the galaxies from a single initial point) the cosmic development began some 20 billion years ago due to the explosion of limitless energy of extreme density. Since, beyond the singularity of this beginning, empirically describable conditions can no longer be identified, this may present the possibility of having recourse to a transcendent cause. However, this consequence would only apply if there were an explanation why this matter came into existence from nowhere in the first place, and not only how, as a result of the constancy of its inceptive conditions, it has developed into its present form.

In contrast to this, Hawking proposes another theory. He combines quantum mechanics with Einstein's General Theory of Relativity. According to this theory, space and time form a non-infinite four-dimensional space without singularities and limits, finite like the surface of the earth. Hence, the world would be finite but unlimited. So, he argues, if the universe is completely enclosed in itself and can be explained by a uniform theory, then God the Creator is superfluous as a final hypothesis for the explanation of the world.

But at least Hawking poses the question of why matter took the trouble to exist anyway. He thus confirms—perhaps unconsciously—the basic difference between the natural scientific query into the empirical conditions of the cosmos and life, on the one hand, and the philosophical query into "why is there any being at all instead of nothing at all," as well as the theological knowledge, on the other hand, that the self-understanding of man in his personhood and the enquiry into the substance and fulfillment of the human quest for meaning and hope are only illuminated by the light of a transcendent Personhood that is not a cause in the empirical-objective sense, but rather, in a transcendentally effective sense, as the free Author of the world and man.

# THE BELIEF IN GOD
# THE CREATOR IN
# BIBLICAL TESTIMONY

The belief in divine creation only acquires its own character over the course of its historical development. This belief corresponds to the various phases of the revelation narrative and reflects the experience of belief both of Israel and the early church. The refocused reflections and reinterpretations find their respective literary expression in the OT and NT.

Viewed in chronological and substantial terms, statements regarding the creation in the OT fall into roughly three groups: 1. The pre-exilic testimonies, 2. The post-exilic creation theology (primarily the Priestly Document and Deutero-Isaiah), and, finally, 3. The creation statements found in the later wisdom literature.

## 1. The Creation Belief in the Old Testament

### a) Pre-exilic testimonies

What is commonly referred to as the Yahwistic narrative of "paradise and the fall of man" from 1000 BC (Gen 2:4b-3:24) is not intended as a descriptive report of the beginnings of the world and man in an empirical sense. The purpose of the literary genre of historical etiology is to enable the reader to interpret his current experience of God and the state of the world by directing his attention to their all-formative beginnings. The knowledge value of this theologically drawn inference is based on the encounter in the present with God in his Word and, hence, proves to be an aspect of God's self-revelation.

However, human knowledge has no direct access to God's creative activity. This is why the message in substance is conveyed analogously to the pious mind in human language and in a narrative sequence of images.

When the author avails himself of human narrative traditions from the world of the Near East, it is by no means his intention to encourage a mythical interpretation of human existence and certainly not to encourage a mythologizing discourse on God. To the contrary, these narratives, taken from mythologizing religions, have been substantially demythologized and their essence, theologized. The hermeneutical key is the belief in Yahweh, the God of Israel, who reveals himself as the Creator of the world and man in the very existence of the world, its order and its wise preparation as an environment for human beings.

The divergence from the mythological-religious ideas of the origin of the world does not consist in the way Yahweh is utilized as a world-creating God but rather in how Yahweh himself determines his divine relation to the world. Yahweh is not one god among others. He alone possesses the essence of the divinity, and, where their complete nullity is not revealed, he demotes the gods of mythology to elements of his own creation.

Yahweh, God the Creator, is always the subject. He is not a predicate to an all-encompassing cosmos. In relation to the world, he is almighty in his action, realizing everything he wills.

This Yahwistic text, however, does not provide any developed theological reflexion on the belief in creation.

Individual references are provided in some hymns of praise to Yahweh in the pre-exilic literature. He performs his miraculous deeds in history. Among these are also that he created the earth, the heavens, plants, animals and man (cf. Ps 19:2; Gen 14:19, 14:22, 24:3; 1 Kgs 8:12; Jer 5:22–24, 27:5, 31:35 f.; Ezek. 28:13).

God's creative activity as a force in history is present to the very ends of the earth, the summits of the mountains, the depths of the oceans, to the realm of the dead. Natural forces must tremble when he appears (Am 9:2–4). The natural cycle of the seasons between summer and winter, between day and night, sowing and harvesting are also guaranteed by God as long as the earth exists (Gen 8:22). He prescribed the path of the sun. It was he who separated the land from the sea (Jer 5:22–24).

A clear statement about the creation can be found Jer 27:5. The emphatic "It was I" testifies to God's self-revelation:

> It was I who made the earth, human being and beast on the face of the earth, by my great power, with my outstretched arm; and I can give them to whomever I think fit.

## b) The Israelite Creation Theology Found in P and Deutero-Isaiah

In connection with many creation statements, what also stands out is the terminology. The *bara* concept is used both to describe God's historical deeds as well as his acts towards nature. Israel, God's people itself is his creature, and Israel's belief is his work (cf. Exod 34:10; Ps 51:12).

Despite all the descriptive (anthropomorphic) imagery, God's deeds must remain clearly incomparable with the way humans behave, act and speak. The image of Yahweh, the potter who makes a work from clay (cf. Jer 18:6; Isa 29:16, 45:9, 64:7; Wis 15:7; Rom 9:21), is not intended as a mythological description of God's craftsmanship. In substance, what is meant is the total dependence of man, its existence, its nature, in its historical course and in the realization of its freedom.

The incomparability of God's activity in nature and in history is expressed in the concept *bara* (Gen 1:1; Isa 42:5) that can only have God as its subject. Increasingly, this word is used as a special concept for God's creative activity.

For this purpose the Septuagint never uses the Greek word δημιουργεῖν (*demiourgeîn*) but rather in most cases ποιεῖν (*poieîn*). The Vulgate translates this with *facere*. This is why, in the Creed, the Christian professes his faith in God, the *factor coeli et terrae*. In the NT divine activity is expressed as κτίζειν (*ktízein*). Man is called κτίσις (*ktísis*). What is meant here is specifically not the work of the craftsman but rather both will and immediate execution, similar to an absolute ruler whose mere command was able to create a city.

The hymn of creation Gen 1:1–2:4a contained in what is known as the Priestly Document (P) was written in the Babylonian exile (in the sixth and fifth centuries). The intellectual performance represents a theological accomplishment of the highest order. The basic assertion is contained in the sweeping heading:

In the beginning God created heavens and earth. (Gen 1:1)

Although Israel's creation belief is not recorded and expressed here in the sense of later theology with precise philosophical categories, it does portend the central constitutive moments of the biblical knowledge of God and the belief in the creation. Hence, they can also be specified by name in the categories of a theological system. The essential individual aspects are:

(1.) God is the sovereign subject of his creative activity. Only God can create. God's creative activity reveals both his omnipotence and goodness to man, who is capable of grasping the world in terms of his relationship to God (cf. Rom 1:18–20). God is a free agent in respect to the world. He is not a predicate of the world and is not demiurgically tangential to the world process or dependent on it.

(2.) The result of the act of creation is the created world as a whole and in relation to its Creator: "heaven and earth."

(3.) The *bara*-activity of God the Creator is not the shaping of an already existing matter or the transformation of pure potentialities into reality. Even if the concept of *creatio ex nihilo* does not appear until later (cf. 2 Macc 7:28: God made everything from nothing, and created humankind in the same way"), it is still implicitly expressed even in the earliest testimonies. This involves an analytic judgment: The concept for Yahweh's creative act also contains the descriptor *ex nihilo*.

The concept "nihil" doubtless suggests the influences of Hellenistic philosophy. However, in the context of the belief in creation it carries another connotation. As in the Aristotelian axiom *ex nihilo nihil fit*, what is really meant by nihil is materia prima. This is pure potential which cannot take on an actual form without an efficient cause. The terminology of Hellenistic education and philosophy, which in part also found its way into the biblical and, later, into the formulation of the Church's Creed had to be substantially transformed. This is the only manner available to express the belief in creation, a manner which was completely foreign to all of Greek philosophy. God the Creator, however, does not in any way stand in juxtaposition to an independent prime matter, i.e., a sort of elemental stuff or realm of potentialities, that had to wait for its formation or realization.

Instead, the concept *creatio ex nihilo* is intended to express the uniqueness of God's creative activity. All reality, in its being, its fundamental existence and form, in the ground of its reality and potentiality, the result of God's free will.

Hence, the psalmist can say: "For he spoke and it came to be, commanded, and it stood in place" (Ps 33:9). This act of God, that has no need for any prerequisite or precondition apart from itself, can virtually become the divine name under which he reveals himself: "God..., who gives life to the dead and calls into being what does not existhttp://www.usccb.org/bible/romans/4 - 53004017-k" (Rom 4:17).

Man's creaturely knowledge is refused adequate insight into God's act of creation. Man is only familiar with the act of working an already existing object.

Viewed from God's perspective, however, creation means he realizes the creature by calling it. And through his calling, i.e., through his making it the object of his action, it originates.

Similarly, this is how Eph 1:4 should be understood: "as he [God] chose us in him [Christ], before the foundation of the world [. . .] ." Here, too, calling, choosing and creating are not distinct, chronologically sequential acts. This means: When God creates us, we are the chosen (the "motivation of the creation"), and by his choosing us, we are created. God's revelation thus proves to be the cause of the created existence of things.

(4.) God realizes his act of creation through his Word and his will. The Word is not an instrument distinguishable from God by which he makes the world. In God, Word and will are identical. They state God's personal, subjective and free activity. There is no room for a procedural mixture of God and nature. The NT picks up on the thought of creation through the Word: "All things came to be through him, and without him nothing came to be" (cf. John 1:3). Here the Word is not generally identified with God's immediacy. Instead, it is a hypostatic realization of God's essence in the personal distinction of Father, Son and Holy Spirit. The creation's preservation and purposeful guidance relate not only to God as the world's efficient cause and final cause. God's essential triunity also underlies creation's orientation, lending meaning and revealing meaning (*causa exemplaris*).

(5.) God creates the world "in the beginning." Time and space do not exist in any sort of objective or logical manner prior to the creation of the world. They are the characteristics, dimensions of the created reality in which the world also becomes visible to man and gives him orientation. Time and space, however, are not "between" God and the world in order to designate a distance. On the contrary, the act of creation establishes the world's orientation, surpassing both time and space, towards God, from whom it originates and to whom it shall return. God is manifestly present as the

Creator everywhere and anytime, in every being. Hence, theology refers to how God brings forth the world in an instant (*in instanti*). A successive act of creation would correspond to the setting up of a house by a master planner in a sequence of distinct construction phases. But the act of creation is as indivisible as God himself. It is not the creation which occurs successively, but rather the created world which, naturally and historically, unfolds successively. The *creatio continua* is identical with the original creatio ex nihilo and designates only the continuing reality and presence of the timeless act of creation and, hence, God himself in the world as a whole as well as in individual evolving processes, in the individuation and personification of man and in the history of human freedom.

(6.) The existence of the world and all its individual things is a revelation of God's essential goodness. These things are, in their reality and their essence, good (Gen 1:31). Evil is not a created substance and, hence, not a manifestation of a dark side of God or of an evil divine principle. Evil should not be confused with the contingency and finality of the creation and does not follow inevitably from it. Moral evil can only arise when a created free will itself turns away from God, from his purpose. But it does not exist as a creature but consists in the will's abandonment of the pursuit of goodness. Evil is manifested in the entangled connections and interconnections of physical misfortune.

(7.) Man's self-knowledge as a creature and the knowledge of the infinite superiority of God the Creator lead him to God as the Holy Mystery, the "hidden God" (Isa 45:15). But man knows he conjoins with his Creator by approaching him with prayer, praise, gratitude and respect (Ps 8; 95; 104). Humanity's responsive and glorifying devotion to God is shared by all other creatures: Heaven and earth praise the glory and honor of God (Isa 6:3; Rev 4:11).

(8.) The belief in creation (protology) is always intertwined with the history of salvation and eschatology.

Especially Deutero-Isaiah (Isa 40–45) supplies a radicalization and summary of the Old Testament belief in creation and is also open to the eschatological, messianic future. Yahweh alone is God. All the gods of the pagans are nothingness. Only Yahweh is the Creator and, hence, he alone is the Redeemer. God is the beginning and the end, the A and Ω of the world, the first and the last (Isa 41:4, 44:6, 48:12).

In Trito-Isaiah there is an imminently consistent expectation of a new creation, a consummating reestablishment of the world, a new heaven and a new earth (Isa 65:17, 66:22; Rev 21:1).

### c) Creation in the Wisdom Literature

Since the Hellenization of the Near East and like many ancient peoples, Israel is familiar with a wise insight which ensues from reasoned observation of natural phenomena, historical events and daily life. The extensive scope of interpretation, however, remains a matter of historical belief in salvation. This means: "The fear of the Lord is wisdom, (Job 28:28; Prov 1:7, 9:10; Sir 1:11–21, 19:20). The order of the world by measure, number and weight reflects God's superior wisdom, just as an admirable structure reflects the superior skills of the architect.

In the personal life of the devote, God's wisdom is also revealed as the superior control and guidance in the destiny of individuals, just as God also retains the entirety of world affairs in his sovereign control and guidance. God alone provides for everything and everyone (Job 38–42; Wis 7:21, 9:9, 12:1; Sir 24:1–6; Prov 3:18 f, 8:22–31).

Wisdom is an attribute of God (Job 28:12–27; Bar 3:12). In other passages, wisdom may appear as God's first creation that was active as an advisor in the creation of the world. It appears personified (as a literary figure of speech), to illustrate God's reasoning (Wis 7:22–8:1; Prov 8:1–21, 9:1–6; Sir 24:1–24). All in all, the wisdom refers to God's continuously ordering and guiding divine presence. On the other hand, it can also expose the foolishness of the godless.

Those who let themselves be guided by wisdom, the Word and the Spirit of God must also know the world in its perfection. The wise attain to a knowledge of God as the [genuinely] real being [the one who is] (Wis 13:1). God's existence and salvific will can be concluded from the greatness and beauty of created things (Wis 13:5; cf. Rom 1:19 f.; Acts 14:17). This is also the basis of the biblical definition of idolatry. Pagans and fools are those who confuse what has been created with God and worship it as holy instead of the Creator. By praying to created things, stars, animals and human beings, they debase God's truth. God convicts them of their foolishness and godlessness (cf. Wis 11:15, 12:24, 13:10 f.; Ps 106:20; cf. Rom 1:18–25).

## 2. Creation Statements in the New Testament

### a) The Belief in Creation in the Earthly Life of Jesus

Jesus identifies God, who he exclusively calls his Father and whose Son he reveals himself to be, as God the Creator, the "Lord of heaven and earth" (Luke 10:21; Matt 11:25). In his annunciation he calls upon the "beginning of creation" (Mark 10:6, 13:19; Matt 13:35, 19:8, 24:21, 25:34; Luke 11:50). The creative will is considered a standard and a yardstick of the religious and ethical grievances of his time. The belief in creation is also associated with Jesus's promulgation of the arrival of the kingdom of God. In the signs pertinent to Jesus, the healing of the ill, the triumph over the demonic powers of evil and the taming of the life-threatening forces of nature, Jesus reveals the traits of divine power. God's creative salvific will is revealed in the eschatological messianic deeds of Jesus. In Jesus God acts as the Lord of history and nature, as the salvific and caring God in the destiny of individuals. God's eschatological peace becomes tangible in the peace between people as well as in the healing of man's disturbed material way of living.

The legitimacy of the mission of Jesus is proven by his entitle-
ment to the *bara*-action of God in the creation and salvation history. That is why in the name of Jesus alone, salvation, i.e., God
himself, can be found (cf. Acts 4:12).

Yahweh's creativity is realized soteriologically in Jesus. The destiny of Jesus relevant to salvation, on the cross and in the resurrection, proves itself the complete revelation of God as the Creator
of salvation in nature, in history and in the opening of an indestructible living community of man and God in the "resurrection
of the dead."

## b) The Theocentricity of the Creation

Everything that exists in the heavens and on earth, the visible and
the invisible, has been created by God through his Word and his
will without any need for a previously existing matter or a realm
of potential.

God is the one who calls what does not exist into being (cf.
Rom 4:17, 11:36; 1 Cor 8:6; Eph 3:9; Col 1:16; Acts 4:24, 14:15, 17:24;
Heb 3:4, 4:11; Rev 10:6, 14:7). The world, created together with
its time structure (Rom 1:20; 1 Pet 1:20; Heb 1:10; Eph 1:4; John
17:24) is wholly oriented around God, the Father. The salvific action of the Son finds its conclusion in his submission to the Father
and obedience to him, "so that God may be all in all" (1 Cor
15:28). "For from him and through him and for him are all things.
To him be glory forever" (Rom 11:36; cf. Heb 2:10). A summary
presentation of the New Testament belief in creation is contained
in the Areopagus speech of Paul (Acts 17:22–31). God created everything that is in the heaven and on earth. Man was created to
seek and find God. The Creator is not distant from any man, "for
in him we live, move and have our being." God is not an image
fashioned or composed by human hands and understanding. God
the Creator has established the day of judgment which will be
administered by Jesus Christ, who he also resurrected from death
(cf. Rev 4:8.11, 5:13).

## c) Jesus Christ as the Intermediary of Creation and Redemption

The Christocentric heightening of the belief in creation comprises two aspects: For one, it is the Eternal Word of the Father (John 1:3) or the Eternal Son (Col 1:12–20; Eph 1:3–14; 1 Cor 8:6), the intermediary of the act of creation, as the trinitarian relation to the creation shows; for another, Jesus, the Son of God made man, is the Redeemer who orients the created world towards its soteriological and eschatological perfection:

---

"Yet for us there is one God, the Father, from whom all things are and for whom we exist, and one Lord, Jesus Christ, through whom all things are and through whom we exist" (1 Cor 8:6).

"He is the image of the invisible God, the firstborn of all creation. For in him were created all things in heaven and on earth, ... all things were created through him and for him. He is before all things, and in him all things hold together. . . . For in him all the fullness was pleased to dwell and through him to reconcile all things for him." (Col 1:15–20, see also Eph 1:3-14; Heb 1:1–3: "He is the refulgence of his glory, the very imprint of his being, and who sustains all things by his mighty Word. . . .)

---

## d) The Pneumatological Mediation of the Belief in Creation

The soteriological acts of Jesus usher in a reconstitution of the creation (cf. 2 Cor 5:17; Gal 6:15). Through Christ and the Spirit man is renewed in the image of his Creator (cf. Col. 3:10) and lives in true righteousness and holiness (cf. Eph 4:24; Luke 1:75). The Spirit of God "which resurrected Jesus from the dead" lives in the believer (Rom 8:11). God brings about the resurrection from the dead through Christ's creative Spirit in the baptized person. Still, along with all of creation, the baptized await their adoption, the revelation of the glory of God when those who "have the first fruits of the Spirit" are revealed in Christ by the redemption of their bodies as the children of God (cf. Rom 8:23).

### e) The Eschatology of Creation

It is the mediation of Christ which transforms the promise of the world's re-creation in the messianic age into a reality (cf. Isa 65:17, 66:22). Given that the creation was God's protological salvific activity, the end and perfection of the world and history are also a salvific event. They bring about the final revelation of God's creative will. A reduction to a cosmologically conceived end of the world is ruled out. The perfection of the creation at the second coming of Christ does not lead to a merger of God and the world but to the perfection of the enduring personal partner in love (for this reason the eschatological image of bridegroom and bride). In the "new heaven and new earth" (Rev 21:1–7) all of creation, through God's people ("the holy city," "the new Jerusalem," "the bride"), animated by the power of the Spirit calls:

> The Lord has established his reign, our God, the Ruler of the whole of creation. Let us rejoice and be glad and give him glory. For the wedding day of the Lamb [Christ] has come, his bride [the Church] has made herself ready. (Rev 19:6 f.)

III

# THE FORMATIVE DEVELOPMENT
# OF THE CREATION TEACHING
# IN THE HISTORY OF THEOLOGY

## *1. In Patristics*

### a) The Apologists of the Second Century

The universal horizon of truth of the Christian faith impelled the apologists in the second century towards a positive mediation of the biblical confession of faith in God with the idea of God provided by the rational theology of Hellenistic culture. An unmediated abrupt claim of the truth of Israel's particular religious tradition was not only impossible as a strategy of proclamation but, most importantly, it stood in contradiction to the claim to universality and rationality inherent in Jewish and Christian belief. However, because creation idea was completely foreign to Greek philosophy and, hence, God was ultimately also unfamiliar as a free and sovereign personhood in relation to the world and in regards to man, the Christian belief in creation necessarily meant a fundamental critique and re-evaluation of the terms also in circulation in Hellenistic culture such as God, cosmos and man, but also reason and reality as well as their whole co-ordinate system.

The recourse to the expression *creatio ex nihilo*, found vividly expressed in 2 Macc 7:28 (cf. Herm., mand. I/1), meant no less in the

41

history of ideas than the first break with the cosmocentric world-view of pagan antiquity. God is not a demiurgical artisan (Plato). He is not the first unmoved mover (Aristotle). He is not pantheistically or theopanistically bonded with the cosmos through an emanation of being from its original unity into the polymorphism of its appearances in its lowest materialization in matter (Neoplatonism). Unlike the systems of the Platonic dualism or stoic monism, God is in relation to the world a free agent. He encompasses everything. He is not contained by the cosmos or by human thought. God is not a predicate of a divine cosmos. He is neither really integrated into the world process nor dialectically or logically joined with it in a higher unity.

In contrast to the polytheistic folk religion, the apologists draw from the emerging philosophical teaching of God's absolute world transcendence, which, however, is not synonymous with the Christian concept of God's transcendence. In this context, the concept "God" is formed by the pure negation of all the characteristics which determine the world. He is beyond any contact with the world and matter. But assuming he is the foundation of the world as the unmoved mover or the demiurge necessitates a system of mediations and mediators. Between the material world and the eternal God, the Logos or World Spirit appears as the mediating principle. The apologists pick up on this philosophical idea of the logos and associate it with the biblical view of Jesus Christ, God's Son and Logos, who is encountered in the NT not only as the Redeemer but also as the Mediator of Creation. The Word or the Son (prior to the incarnation) emanates from God, for the creation and the governance of the world (Justin Martyr 2 apol. 6; dial. 61; Athenagoras, leg. 8; Theophilus of Antioch, Autol. 2,10.22). The question remains open whether the Logos, independent of the creation, is eternally created by the Father, and is thus in substance identical with him (cf. the problem of *homooúsios* of the Son in the dispute over Arianism). This intermingling of the procession of the Son from God and his generation as a Mediator of creation also leaves unclear whether the procession with creation and his appearance at the incarnation only constitutes the Logos when the moment of hypostasis and the divine Person arrives (cf. the question of an essential or merely salvation historical subordinationism in the Christology of the pre-Nicene Fathers of the Church). This still unexplained theological concept does not exclude second century theologians' recognition— as a matter of faith—of the distinction between Father, Son and Holy Spirit as well as the pre-existence and eternal divinity of the Son and the Holy Spirit (cf. Athenagoras, leg. 10).

The central problem of these attempts to resort to theological cosmology and metaphysics to convey the Christian belief in divine creation consists in how creation theology as a whole is pushed aside by God's self-revelation in salvation history and is reduced to a kind of monotheistic cosmology. Hence, the difficulty of conveying the image of God and his attributes by a renunciation in respect to the world (detachment from the suffering of the world, apatheia, impassibility, self-sufficiency, etc.) with the biblical understanding of God, where God in the very act of creation reveals himself as the God of salvific will, of personal encounter and love and as the personally approachable partner in the history of human freedom and search for salvation.

## b) The Unity of Salvation History in Creation and Redemption according to Irenaeus

The dualistic view of the gnosis had assumed two final principles or divinities, the evil god of creation as the Author of the material world and, hence of evil, and the good god of redemption as the Author of the Spirit and goodness. Against this metaphysical dualism, Irenaeus of Lyons asserted the unity of the created world and, thus, also the essential goodness of material reality. Because there are no two final principles or gods, but rather only one God, the unity of creation and redemption (salvation history) is, for this reason, also the proof of God's unity and the uniqueness and vice versa.

Irenaeus also overcomes the duality of creation and salvation history which had become a tangible cause for alarm in the writings of the apologists, thus also overcoming reduction of creation theology to a monotheistic cosmology. Since the one and only God is present from the beginning, the creation and redemption belong together as two phases in the one overall plan of the salvation's realization. In this plan God not only pursues one purpose, the perfection of man in the "apotheosis through grace or in communion with God's life." The purpose of creation does not consist of God creating humanity to free himself of his solitude or to enlarge from emptiness into fullness. God has no need for man. He creates him as the recipient of his good deeds (haer. IV, 14). So the reason for the creation is God's self-giving love, which has no need for gain, and only desires to communicate its own inexhaustible plenitude. In this sense, God is undemanding (cf. the Greek axiom of *apatheia*). Unlike Greek philosophy, however, what is meant here is not isolation from the world in a negative sense, but rather the contrary, what is meant is a love which magnanimously gives of itself. It is possible because God brings forth the world as a creation designed to be in relation to him.

If the goal consists in God's imparting of himself in becoming man, then the original Christocentricity of creation, revealed in the incarnation, can also be seen in the beginning and the end. Such is the historical Jesus, the incarnated Logos of the Father, the ultimate goal of creation. He is proven to be the fundamental cause of the creation, the archetype from which man was created in God's image and likeness and exists as a personally accessible partner (cf. the trinitarian understanding of Gen 1:26 "Let *us* make man in our image, similar to *us*..."; cf. Barn. 6:12).

In terms of salvation history and eschatology, Jesus Christ embodies the identity of the God of creation and redemption. In him, the inner benevolence and goodness of all spiritual and material creation is revealed.

Sin cannot tear apart the intimate relationship between creation and the gift of grace. Through the forgiveness of sins, God's salvific will merely takes another path towards the achievement of his purpose.

In this sense, Irenaeus takes up the ideas expressed in Acts 3:21 concerning a restoration of everything (ἀποκατάστασις, *recapitulatio omnium*), which in the end is enacted by the Father in Jesus Christ.

The relationship of the creation to the redemption is similar to that of the beginning of a process which, by passing through a phase of growth, strives towards its outer perfection. However, this should not be understood as an organologic-evolutionary process, but rather as a maturation and development of personal freedom in the drama of the history of God and man.

Irenaeus was able to overcome the gnostic dualism of a God of creation and a God of redemption, an evil and a good nature in man, of a created nature and a salvation historical event by a salvation historical (economic) understanding of the Trinity. Yet this merely historically structured narrative of God's salvific deeds does not suffice to resolve all the related metaphysical questions such as the relationship of God's absolute being to finite reality of the creation, of God's omnipotence to human freedom, as well as of "nature of evil."

## c) The Attempt to Mediate the Belief in Creation Rationally by Posing the Metaphysical Question of the Origin (Clement, Origen)

The Alexandrians Clement and Origen sought (as did earlier the Jewish theologian and philosopher Philo of Alexandria, who died in AD 65) to transpose biblical belief into the categories of Platonic philosophy, thus, to convey it in terms of Hellenistic rationality. In the midst of this authoritative dialectic of continuity and contradiction we must recognize, in turn, how the biblical teaching was not twisted to fit the categories of Hellenistic philosophy, but rather that these categories themselves were critically revised in view of the constants in the Bible's understanding of God, perception of reality and image of man.

In his main opus, *De principiis*, Origen distinguishes between the binding statements of belief (as stated in the *regula fidei*) and their theological conception with the help of antiquity's cosmology and natural theology (what is important here is the reference to the Platonic dialog *Timaeus*, the authors Aristotle, Theophrastus, Galenus, Plinius and Cicero).

Belief unshakably holds: God the Creator called all things into being from nothingness and ordered them. He is identical with the God of all the righteous, starting with Adam, Abel and Abraham. Jesus Christ is the Son of God, born of the Father before all creation. The world was created through him by the Father. It has a beginning in time and an end in time.

Man is a creature endowed with freedom and reason and, hence, the author and master of his deeds (in contrast to being determined by fate or the influence of the planets). He is not constrained to be at the mercy of the devil. Man has a free will as a pre-requisite for acting in a manner which is good or evil. That is why there is wage, merit and punishment.

The devil is not created as an evil substance. His wickedness consists in his turning his freely created will away from God.

In his metaphysical penetration of the belief in divine creation, Origen developed individual aspects of the creation doctrine that have remained significant in the history of theology:

### *The idea of simultaneous creation*

Following the example of Philo, the biblical creation story is not interpreted as a realistic report. In substance, it wants to be seen as the representation of an act of God beyond the realm of time. The act, identical with God, through which the world is created and maintained (*creatio continua*), cannot be measured in days and hours. Corresponding to the biblical wording "He who lives for ever created all things together—*creavit omnia simul*" (Sir 18:1 Vg.), eternity is an essential characteristic of God, one which he also does not lose in his free relationship to the world. So the act of creation is not a divine activity which can be measured chronologically, it is atemporal. Of course, this does not exclude; it includes how the world itself can also exhibit an evolution of natural phenomena and a history of human freedom.

Due to this radical differentiation of eternity as an essential characteristic of God and time as a signature of the created world, the eternal procession of the Logos from the Father can also be in principle differentiated from the chronological procession of creation from God.

### The inclusion of the theory of ideas

The forms of things are considered as the realization of original concepts in the Spirit of God (exemplarism). Things are the copies of the ideas already existing in God. They have their archetype in the divine Logos and, hence, finally, also their purpose. This relationship of the world in its inner constitutional moments to God's inner reality can be expressed even more precisely by the Platonic idea of participation (cf. Gregory of Nyssa, or. catech. V,2). Of course, there arises here a tension between the biblical salvation historical realism and an idealism that sees the created world as somehow the existentially weaker reflection of its archetypically pre-existing ideas in God. Here, the actual being of things could appear as a diminution of their potential being in God's thinking. This problem arose in all Platonic and neo-Platonic representations of the Creator-created relationship (as in Pseudo-Dionysius the Areopagite).

If the egress of the created world from God is a metaphorical repetition and representation of an archetypically eternal procession of the Son from the Father and is also included in his responsive return movement (cf. the egress-regress pattern), then a naturalistic narrative of the creation process (cf. the neo-Platonic principle: *bonum diffusivum sui*) can only be avoided by a positivistic emphasis on God's absolute freedom to act. In the ninth century, John Scotus Eriugena (died in 877) takes up this neo-Platonic view of a link between the procession of the world from God and its purpose in God with the procession of the Son from the Father from his responsive return back to him. The creation was presented as one appearance of God's inner-trinitarian self-differentiation. But that calls into question the independent reality (subsistence) of the creation. God is then quasi the ground of being of changes in the world (cf. Hegel's idealistic trinity theology and process-phi-losophy in the nineteenth and twentieth centuries). However, this neo-Platonic-Plotinian understanding of the creation doctrine can be countered by saying that the original relations in God which account for the personhood of the Father, the Son and the Holy Spirit are integral to God's essence. The world does not exist in contrast to him because God is internally distinctive in the three persons but because God himself wills this distinctiveness from the world, which exists as a reality whose essence is in substance differ-ent than his and which, through the agency of man, is in a personal relationship with him (not in the sense of a natural process).

The Lateran Synod 649 established the undivided Trinity in unity as the principle of divine action and, hence, the cause of the creation (DH 501) in response to a simple parallelization of the inner-trinitarian processions and the procession of the world from God's will following the idea-image scheme as well as the egress-regress scheme. Of course, this does not mean that some abstract divine Nature behind the divine Persons is the Creator. God the Father, alongside whom the Logos and the Pneuma ex-ist coequally, is the author of creation and salvation history and is revealed therein as the triune God.

### The gradation between the spiritual and material worlds

What is problematic is the notion of the spiritual world as genu-ine existence in contrast with a material world that can only be the result of a fall. The pre-existing souls are put into the cre-ated material world to be punished and educated. Inversely, then, redemption means a progressive spiritualization and, finally, the return of the creation to its original condition (cf. the teaching of the *apocatastasis* and its rejection by the magisterium). While Origen, in contrast to gnostic dualism and to neo-Platonic emana-tionism, emphasizes the personal moment of freedom in history—and, hence, there is no evidence of a metaphysical dualism in his writing—Platonic dualism's categorical scheme of the spiritual and sensual worlds, is still stigmatizing. The path of belief and knowledge (Christian gnosis) is a transition from a chronological, ephemeral and vacuous world into the spiritual, everlasting and eternal reality of God. In response to this, however, it should be remembered that at issue is not the transition from the lower to the higher level of existence but rather that man, in the unity of his spiritual-material nature, finds in God not another nature but rather the purpose of his journey and, hence, the perfection of his nature, which is both spiritual and material.

## d) The Creation Theology of Saint Augustine

Augustine developed his creation theology in his disputes with Manichaeism. He shows how Manichaeism, by denying the independence of mind and its distinctiveness from matter, is a form of philosophical materialism. This reduces God to a mere material substance which flows in stages through the world. An essential difference between God and the world is unimaginable and God's freedom and spirituality are abandoned. And man is not considered a spiritual being either. The soul is not a spiritual and free principle of motion. Evil can only be explained naturally as man's inseparable connection with matter, the source of finiteness. Turning to the neo-Platonic philosopher Plotinus (205–270), especially to his *Enneads*, Augustine discovered the primacy of the mind over matter. There is a non-corporeal light which acts as the horizon and cause of all knowledge of the truth. In it God is revealed to us as pure mind. The ascent to God requires liberation from enslavement to material things. This is the only way for us to move from the visible to the invisible. Only God is the fullness of being and the sole truly existing being. Everything else only exists to the extent that it participates in the existence of God.

Everything that exists is good, even matter. Despite the different gradation, being is only delimited from the other being through the different mode of participation in being. Being and being good are identical. Hence, evil cannot acquire its own share in existence, but only a reduction in substance or its suppression in the order of being (*privatio boni*). The aspects that ensue from this for the theology of creation are:

### God created the world from nothing

According to the materialistic notion of God put forward by the Manichaeans, God is a light–substance, and man participates in it. This introduces a mortal element into God. The notion of God disintegrates. But if God is being in eternity, immutability and oneness, then the world in its reality and essence must be considered as distinct in its reality and essence. This means: It was called into being out of nothing. An assumption of previously existent matter (already formed or as pure potentiality) contradicts God's sovereignty. Since only God is true being, he alone can lend finite being to matter as to spiritual forms and, thus, bring about their existence. But why did God create heaven and earth? The answer can only be: "Because he wanted to" (De Genesi contra Manich. I, 2, 4). Since there is no motive outside of God for his action and God is, on the contrary, identical with his will, for us, in the freedom of his creation of the world, God remains unfathomable.

But God's will is also identical with his goodness. In the creation he wants to communicate his goodness to things and reveal himself in them. The world, in its existence, its order and its purposeful movement is a revelation of God's self-giving love.

### The creation has a beginning in time

In response to the Manichaeans' question, what did God do before the creation, Augustine answers, that prior to the creation there was neither time nor space (De Genesi contra Manich. I, 2, 4). Time designates the form in which the created exists. To the extent that the created differs in substance from the Creator, it is also essentially different inasmuch as God's form of existence, inaccessible to us, surpasses any chronological sequence and spatial separation. This is what we call God's eternity without knowing univocally what eternity is in itself (cf. Augustine's highly significant philosophy of time: conf. XI, civ. XI and XII).

Similar to Origen, Augustine also defends a simultaneous creation. (However, this doctrine is unrelated to the natural philosophical theory, widespread in the nineteenth century prior to Darwin, of the constancy of the species.) The biblical description of creation in six days must be understood in a metaphorical and figurative sense. A literal understanding must lead to a contradiction in the concept of God (Gen. ad litt. 4, 33). On the contrary, the six days are intended to show the unfolding of world history over time (they are also the background of a philosophy of history of the six ages). Time is part of man's inner experience, to the extent that only the soul can measure time by means of memory in accordance with its span back into the past and forwards into the future (*distentio animi*). But time is also part of the determination of things themselves that could never realize their being all at once. Things did not exist within time, enveloped by it as though it were an objective measure, Augustine continues. They themselves are internally chronologically structured. That does not distinguish them from God in terms of a third external cosmological factor but in terms of their inner being.

God himself is indivisibly present. He has no need to mediate by means of a memory what might be called his past nor to move towards something called a future. He is therefore necessarily outside of time. Since the world does not exist at all outside of its creation, God is also not tied to it. By being created by God it has a qualified relation to God as creation through its chronological and spatial characteristics. That is why God created everything *in instanti*. But everything that exists in time is in direct relationship with the act of creation and, hence, to God himself, at any one time in its existence.

### God created matter and the spiritual forms

Augustine understands the narrative of the creation of heaven and earth as the bringing forth of the spiritual and sensual world. Matter is merely a substrate that without form returns immediately into nothingness. Hence, it exists concretely only as formed matter.

What can be recognized is only the composite of those things created as matter and form.

To explain the origin of forms, i.e., the spiritual and indestructible substance of things, Augustine turns to the Platonic theory of ideas. He transports ideas into the mind of God. The concrete forms have their real existence where they are joined with matter, in things. But they also have an ideal existence in God's Logos, i.e. in the eternal mediator of the whole creation. Even after they exist as forms concretely with matter in the world they do not precipitate out of their ideal being in the Logos.

When God forms matter into concrete things, matter always harbors a movement towards form. But the spiritual form moves towards its ideal prime cause in God's Logos. The whole creation is characterized by an inner movement from matter to form, from form to idea, and from the idea to God. The pre-human things existed in God's idea only as species and types. Man is conceived in God as an individual. In the world there may be a bounty of traces of the trinitarian God. Man, however, as a personal, spiritual form is in God's image and likeness. That is why man, by virtue of his soul, his spiritual form, is created to be indestructible and immortal. It achieves this purpose through the mediation of the salvation historical acts of the God become man, the idea and likeness of all creation.

Augustine addressed himself to the problem of the continuous creation of new living beings. He differentiates those who from the outset are consummated in their form (the angels, the earth, fire, water, air and the soul of man) from other living beings who are only created as their primordial germs (such as the Adam's body and the bodies of his descendants proceeding from him). These are the original seeds which fill the whole world (*rationes seminales*, with a certain similarity with today's understanding of the genetic code as the bearer of biological evolution). From them proceed, in a mysterious way, the corresponding forms and join together with them into individual living beings. But God alone remains the origin of all forms. He alone grants growth to the primordial germs. Parents physically already bear within themselves the primordial seeds of the child, but it is God who creates the new man by granting growth and the addition of the soul as the spiritual form of this matter.

## Substantiality, spirituality and immortality of the human soul

Augustine starts from the inner experience that the soul in its decisions is the foundation of the ethical personality of man. In his inner experience of himself man grasps himself both in his oneness as well as in the distinction between his soul and body. He experiences his body as being confined to one place. Mediated by the soul, man grasps his body within the three-dimensionality of the world. But his corporeal experience is not accompanied by man's experience of inwardness and self-givenness in his mind and free will that we call the soul. The soul, in an extentionless realization, comprehends itself immediately as mind. It knows immediately that it is alive and that its life is thought (trin. X,13). It understands itself as the organizational and actional principle of the body as a whole. The soul is not limited to one place in man, it is present throughout the whole body and in all its limbs. The soul needs the body as its medium for the material world. Inversely, however, the body is mediated back by the soul, its spiritual form, into God's world of ideas. Hence, the soul means participation in God as life. So, ultimately, God is the sole principle of the soul in its existence, in its actualization and in its purposeful movement. The soul exists through participation in the eternal ideas of the truth and goodness of the holy God. Because of this background and this constitutive relationship it is immortal in particular in contrast to the corruptibility of the body.

It proves to be a substance of its own (= reality principle, not a physical substrate) that cannot be reduced to a vegetative and animal life principle. This is why it is not the corruption of the body but exclusively God who can remove being from the soul and lead man into nothingness. But since the soul is created by God as a spiritual substance, death, as a consequence, is described as a separation of the immortal soul from its body. Nevertheless, death is a process in the spiritual-personal dimension of man and not merely the decease of the body from the soul. Yet the soul is not annihilated but preserved for the divinely planned resurrection of man in his new spiritual-corporeal existence.

In contrast to the Platonic talk of the immortality of the soul, in Augustine, the nature of the soul is described through its immediate creation relationship to God. The soul is the specific spiritual creation in which God reveals himself as the origin and simultaneously the perfection of the creation. Man is created according to the ideal image in God. He is also consummated in the Logos made man. The soul with its basic functions of memory, reason and will, is already endowed with an image to know the divine triunity, toward which the soul advances as its goal, acting knowingly and consciously.

## The created will as an external condition of its orientation towards evil

According to Augustine, there can be no substantial evil in a good creation. Evil exists only when a created will turns away from the highest good and towards the lesser good in the sense of absolutizing and deifying the creation. The created goods are to be "utilized" (*uti*) while God alone can be "enjoyed" by man in love (*frui*). The evil will, which has turned its back on the good, performs the evil deed, which consists of theft or in a privation of the good (*privatio boni*). The evil has no positive cause of its own by which it is moved. God is the immediate cause of the created will's capacity to desire. But he does not bring about the actual desire of the will to renounce the good and, hence, God himself.

Gnostics and Manichaeans ask: Should not God have created the creaturely will such that it would always have to pursue goodness? A compulsive turning of a created will to goodness, however, would be nothing less than the annulment of its freedom and, hence, its nature. A natural-material determination is the opposite of a causality in freedom. The good as the goal of the will is more than merely the liberation from and absence of the detracting effects of an infringement of the world order; it is the unification with God in love. God risks or plans a possibly self-perverting crea-turely will for the sake of the greatest purpose of all, the perfection of the freedom created in love. However, a perverted will cannot annul the goodness of the creation itself and create evil in terms of substance. A perverted will cannot stand in the way of the world's overall orientation towards unity with God and, thus, in the way of God's salvation plan. It can only exclude itself from the over-all dynamic of the world and, hence, stray from its own purpose. Hence, "God's punishment" is not the revenge of a disappointed lover who must let off steam by enforcing sanctions and causing damage. Instead, it results as the inner consequence of the freedom which excludes God. In the "punishment" God reveals his righ-teousness and his goodness as the origin and goal of creation and the dynamic relatedness of will of the created individual's will and the goodness that is his salvation.

## 2. The Creation Theme in the Theology of the Early Middle Ages

### a) The Neo-Platonic Creation Theology of John Scotus Eriugena

Influenced by Pseudo-Dionysius the Areopagite, Maximus the Confessor and the Neoplatonist Proclus, Eriugena (810–877) gives the concept of creation a decisively Plotinian dimension in his work entitled *De divisione naturae*. A central point is the last meta-physical difference of the One and the Many. The one divine prime cause is mediated into the multiplicity of worldly things via emana-tion, which results in the creation of a hierarchical empire of being corresponding to the various degrees of participation in the One and the Good following the principle *bonum diffusivum sui*. Hence, all of reality is infused and related to each other by an underlying pattern: specifically the emergence from oneness into multiplicity and the return of multiplicity into the One and the Good. (From a Christian perspective this idea can only be adapted if God is thought of as being outside of this process as a free author and if he is not included into the series of emanations.)

Associated with this is the tradition of *theologia negativa* and the tradition of a correspondingly neo-Platonically influenced Christian mysticism (such as in Eriugena, Meister Eckhart, Jakob Böhme, Baruch de Spinoza, Angelus Silesius, Johann Gottlieb Fichte). Characteristic of this theology is a feeling of oneness with the eternal beyond a hypostatizing, projecting view of God (what is known as the metaphysics of substance of rationalism), and beyond a cosmological metaphysics as in the case of deism or physico-theology.

Eriugena wants to connect the creation to God by logically linking the trinitarian processions, the procession of the world, external to God, and the world process born by God. The fundamental metaphysical category of the One and the many can also (with Proclus) be aligned with the primordial universal as well as with the special and the individual. If one removes hypothetically the special characteristics and individualities that are factually given with the One/general, pure being collapses in on itself or reveals its emptiness. Only taken together with its differentiation is being a something. Hence, the divine essence includes, in order for it to be conceived as living, the self-differentiation in the process of becoming. First, it is identical with the trinitarian God as a unit which differentiates itself. With the procession of the essentially identical Logos, however, the divine ideas of created things are simultaneously eternally included. Since in the eternal procession of the Son the world also ideally proceeds eternally, the world process, with its disjunction in the things, is integral to the divine self-expression in the Father, self-knowledge in the Word and imbued with love in the form of the Holy Spirit. That is why Eriugena can say

> that God himself is the maker of everything and at the
> same time has become in everything... Thus, only by
> lowering himself out of the transcendency of his nature,
> which is considered non-being, is he created by himself

in the primordial causes and the beginning of every essence and every life, every cognition and all things which the gnostic observation perceives in the primordial causes. (De div. nat. = PhB 86/87, HH 1983, 336)

For this reason, without the creation, indivisibly joined with the procession of the Logos, God would only be general being or the emptiness of nothingness. As God's general being differentiates itself in the world process, the world emerges from nothingness and God, proceeding through the world, obtains to his own fullness.

Nevertheless, in Eriugena's writing, God also always remains aloof from the world so that the accusation of the pantheism, emanationism and theopanism is in its intentions perhaps not altogether justified. The similarity of this neo-Platonic system with Hegel's absolute idealism is striking.

The Synod of Valence (855) condemned the position of Eriugena in the predestination dispute of his age (DH 633). At the Synod of Paris in 1210 and in a decree issued by Pope Honorius III in 1225 his theses were condemned together with those of Amalrich of Benq (deceased 1206, cf. DH 808) and David of Dinant (deceased 1215) pantheizing interpretation of the act of creation. God's transcendence does not remain assured if the created world is identical with God or if God is understood as prime matter and, hence, matter is equated with the self-differentiation of God in the world process and, for this reason, God appears as the physical first cause of the world process. God and the world could not be weighed in an immanent development pattern against each other ontologically, emanationally or dialectically. Nor can God be the *esse formale* of things or their sum.

## b) The Tension between the Metaphysical and Salvation Historical Creation Theology

The members of the school of Chartres (Thierry of Chartres, Bernhardus Sylvestris, John of Salisbury, Guillaume de Conches, Gilbert de la Porrée and others), in their interest in the natural sciences, let themselves be led by the Platonic dialog *Timaeus* to an elucidation of the concept of creation influenced more by natural philosophy and cosmology. A mystical-sacral feeling of the universe reveals in the structure of nature the rule of the divinity. In the "book of nature" it is possible to read and honor God's thoughts (similarities to the mystical apprehension of God in the physico-theology of the seventeenth and eighteenth centuries; Kepler, Newton, and others). In the thirteenth century, the Oxford Franciscan school (Robert Grosseteste, Roger Bacon) designated God as the form of things. In this sense, which draws more on exemplarism, the world is marked by God's radiating goodness that bears and penetrates everything (metaphysics of light).

The theology of the metaphysical thinkers known as the dialecticians (Anselm of Canterbury, Peter Abelard, Peter Lombard) is also less inclined to understand creation in terms of salvation history. Metaphysical understanding attempts to analyze a subject in terms of its inner regularities and structures. The essential, the natural and eternally valid are solely accessible to reason, while the historical and, hence, accidental cannot be the object of science nor of theology. Only through positive revelation information does the Christian know that God is the one author of two internally disparate activities, creation and redemption. An inner relationship of the trinitarian God and creation is no longer clear outside the positive knowledge that the trinitarian God, corresponding to the inner order of the processions of persons, is the one and undivided cause of the creation. But this prepared the way for the isolation of the trinity theology of the creation and salvation history (cf. Lombard, II Sent.).

A creation theology decidedly based on salvation-history and trinitarian reasoning can be found in Hugh of Saint-Victor (1096–1171). In his main opus, *De sacramentis christianae fidei*, he sees the underlying relationship between the *opus conditionis* and the *opus reparationis* as grounded in the unity of the salvific action of the threefold God. Rupert of Deutz (1075/80–1130), in his work *De*

*Trinitate et operibus eius*, grasped the creation in its trinitarian and christocentric context more clearly. Drawing on the Eastern trinity doctrine the Father appears as the origin of the triunity as well as the origin of creation. The creation's inner purpose is to reveal the Son of the Father in order to make its grounding in the Logos knowable. The creation of man to reflect in the image and likeness of God (cf. Gen 1:26) is, thus, equivalent to a promise which does not find its historical fulfillment until the incarnation of the Logos. In commune with the revealed mediator of the whole of creation, man participates in the life of the threefold God and returns to the Father, the origin, the goal and the fullness of all beings and all salvation history

## 3. The Creation Theology of High Scholasticism

### a) The preparation of the high scholastic syntheses in the reception of Aristotle

Thanks to the reception of the writings of Aristotle in the thirteenth century, theology acquired a new set of instruments to comprehend the belief in divine creation in such a rationally consistent way that enabled the elimination of the potential dangers posed by the heresies of an immanent pantheism and a transcendent dualism (cf. the reification of God).

This succeeded primarily by associating the Aristotelian metaphysical principle of causality with the Platonic idea of participation.

If God is the metaphysical cause of the world, then the world is different than God ontologically. As the free and sovereign personhood (*institutor naturae*), he does not stand apart from the world like an object accessible to human thought. Since God as *prima causa transcendens universalis*, by granting participation in his being and life, mediates his own reality to the world, the creation has an inner orientation towards God. God is not an object in the beyond; he is recognized as the secret of the origin and future of the world.

Metaphysical causality stands in the way of a pantheistic mixing of world and God. The participation concept (and the analogy of being) prevents a dualistic juxtaposition of God and the world or a reified beyond in relationship to a here-and-now.

The two most important exponents of this doctrine of creation, that was reformulated drawing on Aristotelian and Platonic categories, are Bonaventura (1221–1274) from the older Franciscan school who leaned more towards Platonism, and Thomas Aquinas (1224/25–1274), who together with his teacher Albert the Great (1193–1280), belonged to the Dominican school. The full reception of Aristotelian philosophy, most importantly, his books on metaphysics and physics (transmitted by the Aristotle commentators Alfarabi, Avicenna, Algazel and, primarily, Averroës, but also by the Jewish philosophers Avicebron and Moses Maimonides), confronted creation theology with three substantial questions:

1. According to Averroës, the world is eternal and has no beginning in time. Matter is also eternal. The world which concretely formed exists because the unmoved mover draws the forms from the world's inexhaustible wealth of matter.

2. Averroës assumes that the one God directly created only the uppermost first intelligence. The lower intelligences (including the lowest of these, man) are created and guided by the higher intelligences. The lower intelligences have no direct relation to God.

3. Finally, the notion was put forward for discussion that individual human persons only possess passive intellect, while active intellect (*intellectus agens*) is, numerically, in all human persons, one. But this active intellect requires the multiplicity of individual human persons because it (as a designation of mankind) cannot be completely exhausted in only one single individual. This active reason never

becomes the property of individual human persons. That is why the individual soul is not immortal. The individual human person only participates in the immortality of the supra-individual soul (of mankind) to a certain degree. This led to the question of whether individual immortality of man is philosophically provable or can be found solely in revelation. In ethical terms, the problem is posed whether it is possible to speak of man's free responsibility or whether we must confirm his resignation to fatalism.

## b) The Creation Theology of Saint Bonaventura

The central creed of faith retains its validity for Bonaventura, as for all Christian theologians: God, the free author of the world, is the origin, center and measure of the world as well as its purpose. Following the three steps steps of *emanatio, exemplaritas* and *reductio*, Bonaventura unfolds his original creation doctrine in analogy to the inner-trinitarian processions and relations (cf. his works *Breviloquium*, Chap. 2; *Collationes in Hexaemeron*).

That is why Aristotle was unable to arrive at an absolute belief in divine creation because he lacked the basis of the belief in the Trinity. In this context, God is merely the mover of the form but not the Creator of materia prima as well. The thought of creatio ex nihilo and the corresponding beginning of the world in time was a notion foreign to Aristotle's system. According to Bonaventura, the being of God is purely spiritual. Hence, God is self-knowledge. In the act of his being he is simultaneously the actual unity of knowing and being known. That is the Father and Son duality that knows and is consummated in the Holy Spirit as an actual unity. At the moment in which the Father knows himself in the Son he also perceives essentially identical expression of his being. The Son or the Word is the perfect image of God's self-knowledge. Son is the Word in which God comprehends himself and speaks. The act of God's self-knowledge, however, is not an empty game. By generating the Word he proves himself fruitful. The Father's

own fertility approaches him as divine eternity in the Son. In this
creative, unlimited wealth of divine life are contained all realities
and possibilities of a world external to God that has been willfully
placed apart.

The thought of the creatio ex nihilo and the beginning of the
world in time means nothing more than that God is in possession
of his own being through himself while the essence of the world is
contingent and finite and exists solely thanks to God's act of free
will and his granting of participation in being.

But the world is not a thing that has been arbitrarily put in place
and has no relationship to God. According to its actuality and potentiality, it is founded in the image of the Father, the eternal Word.
The procession from the Father of the Son, and his grateful answer,
becomes the idea of the movement of created things that proceed
from the art of the Father. The Logos as the self-expression of the
Father is thus the exemplary cause of creation. This is an additional
gift from the Father to the Son, in which he knows himself and
which, in the shared Holy Spirit, he lovingly wills. As God also
knows himself in the creation in the Word and, in the Holy Spirit,
loves, he also impresses on it his trinitarian characteristics. The
world exists as an original metaphor and a richly ordered analogy
of the Trinity. Depending on the level of being, there results in the
individual beings the *imagines trinitatis*: as the shadow of in the in-
animate things (*umbra*), as a trace in living beings (*vestigium*) and
as an image in the created persons (*imago*). Man, whose essence
is spiritually personal and spiritual-cum-corporeal, integrates all
three levels in himself. However, he brings them together in himself in such a way that he must be seen as the unequivocal image
of God. Only man, in his personhood, can make God the object
of his homage. Hence, he is personally related to God, the Father,
the Son and the Holy Spirit. In his existence, his knowledge and
his orientation toward fulfillment in love, man is the image of God.
Through the creative activity of the Father, God is the author of his
existence; he is known in the Son, the essentially identical Word
and the idea of the creation; and he knows God by participating in

God's self-knowledge to the extent that he is loved by God in the Holy Spirit and the bond of love, and is called upon and capable of the love of God as his participation in God's loving oneness.

## c) The Creation Theology of Saint Thomas Aquinas

### *The creation doctrine in the whole of his theology*

Saint Thomas without doubt represents an apex in creation theology. He consistently turns to Aristotelian lines of thought and basic terminology (existence and being; *existentia* and *essentia* (essence); actuality and potentiality; form and matter, the division into transcendent causes of the *causa efficiens* and *causa finalis* and the constitutional principles immanent to being, specifically the *causa formalis* and *causa materialis*).

Being is determined by the transcendentals of the One, True and Good as well as by the ten categories (the substance as the designation of an existing being and the nine types of accidents: quantity, quality, relation, action, passion, time, place, disposition, raiment). But Thomas did not hesitate to correct Aristotle because the philosopher was not familiar with a genuine concept of creation nor, correspondingly, was he familiar with God as a free personhood, who completely determines himself and is sovereign over the creation (eternity and the uncreated nature of prime matter).

Unlike Saint Bonaventura, however, Thomas teaches only the possibility of a creation by God from nothing. It describes the ontological dependence of the world on God's creative positing act. Finally, light can only be shed on the trinitarian and salvifically relevant profundity of the creation in faith, i.e., by illuminated reason and guided by grace. Moreover, Thomas also teaches that nothing suggests that the temporality of the beginning of the world must be provable using reasonable philosophical arguments, just as little as the eternity of the world can be proved philosophically. Indeed, reason, in conceiving the temporal beginning of the world or the world as having no beginning, gets caught in an antinomy (cf. Kant, KrV B 452 ff.). Thomas says, finally, faith establishes that God created the world in the beginning and at the beginning of time (cf. S. th. I q. 46 a. 2).

In the *Summa theologiae* Thomas does not propound his own creation doctrine in the sense of an isolated tractate. It is an integral part of the doctrine of the one God (cf. the commentary on the Sentences, the *Compendium theologiae*, the *Summa contra gentiles* II, a few *Quaestiones disputatae* and the corresponding commentaries on scripture). The first main section of the *Summa* discusses God and the beginning of creation by him; the second main section discusses man and his pilgrimage to God; while the third main section presents Jesus Christ as the God–Man who in a double mediation is from God as the divine Word and, as man, through God, unites God's movement towards man and man's movement towards God.

The doctrine of the one God has three parts: 1. The doctrine of God's existence, essence and operations as well as his knowability and expressibility by created reason (S. th. I qq. 2–26); 2. the procession of the three persons in God (qq. 27–43); 3. the procession of creatures from God in the sense that he is their *principium et finis* (qq. 44–119).

In this third section there are a total of four subsections:

a) In qq. 44–49 Thomas develops the fundamental concept of creation. It is created by a procession of the world from the trinitarian God produced by free creation. Hence, it has the ontic-ontological reason for its existence, its inner meaning and purpose in God as the transcendent *causa efficiens*, *causa exemplaris* and *causa finalis*. This includes the problem of the preservation of the world in existence and tracing back all its orders in the multiplicity of species and individuals to God's unity. Also central is the question of the origin and nature of the morally evil (*Unde malum?*) in a creation that naturally represents the goodness of God.

b) In the qq. 50–64 the doctrine of angels (angelology) is treated with the guiding question of how spiritually gifted creations can burden themselves with sin and accept punishment (demonology).

c) qq. 65–102: The creation of corporeal natures is treated in the sequence of the six days of creation. At the end, there is an extensively detailed anthropology (qq. 75–102). The subject is the substantial unity of the body and soul of man, the soul being the unifying principle, the powers of the soul (intellect, sensuality, and will); the fundamental epistemological question of how an intellect bound to the senses knows the spiritual structure of the material world and how does it know non-sensual realities (the angels), and, finally, God in his purely spiritual reality. Man is thematized in his perfection as substantial form (*perfectio formae*), i.e., as a personal being that must realize itself by acting (*operatio*) freely and, to this extent, is finalized when his nature is consummated in reference to a reality beyond him (*perfectio finis*), which is only possible if God has granted him grace and righteousness.

d) qq. 103–119 treat God's general and special world government and providence as well as the possibility of good angels and angels who have become evil towards people.

### The basic Thomist conception of the creation

The doctrine of the procession of creatures from God as their author and absolute first cause (*causa efficiens*) requires the Thomist concept of God: God's being is his essence. He is real through himself, from himself and for himself (cf. Eph 4:6) (*ipsum esse per se subsistens*). Whatever exists in juxtaposition to God exists through participation in being. Creaturely *existentia* is always inner and essential *ens per participationem*. Corresponding to the different degrees of participation in general being, there arise the finite beings in the multiplicity of genera, species, and individuals. God's subsistent being is by his nature absolutely simple and unique. That is why God alone is the universal and exclusive cause of manifoldly existing beings, that, in conformance with the granting of participation in existence, are individual in their essential characteristics and subsist individually. Since God brings forth the world freely through his own will, the world cannot be a natural emanation from the divine substance or its manner of appearance. The discussion about causality highlights the infinite difference between the world and God. God and the world are not different from each other in light of some third entity. God himself in his infinitude is the infinite difference to the world.

According to Thomas, God bestows the being and form of things in the act of creation (but not in the pantheistic sense of self-differentiation according to which a unity is expressed in the multiplicity of world processes). The general being through which the created things, corresponding to their participation in being, are specified, modified and limited within their essence, and so acquire subsistence, is neither God himself nor a kind of materia prima out of which God forms finite things. General being exists only within the created essences that, through being, come into existence. This is how being, in which creatures participate and through which they exist thanks to God's creative activity, grounds the absolute difference between things and God and a creaturely independence in relation to God. In man this independence resolves into a personal autonomy that embodies the prerequisites of a personal relation with God and communication with him. The substantial form of the human reality of mind and freedom is the primary act through which man subsists. But it is in his activity that he fulfills himself. This is why part of man's nature is an independent self-propelled movement towards the consummating goal that exceeds the potentials of his nature and fulfills them, God himself. Hence, God's creational relationship to man may not be conceived in the reified sense of deism or physico-theology as the relationship of a craftsman to his workpiece.

> The creatureliness of man entails a personal relation-
> ship to God which determines the essence of man in
> his origin and his consummating orientation towards
> God. For this reason nature is oriented towards grace
> and finds its perfection in grace alone. (cf. S. th. I q. 1
> a. 8 ad 2)

Because no matter how strongly the description of the act of creation stresses the absolute difference between the Creator and the creature, with the help of the theory of causality, the inner purposive orientation is made clear with the help of the category of participation. The participation concept says that God as the origin of the creature is also most intimately existent within things. Of course, this should not be seen objectively and quantitatively. To the contrary, God is within things in the same sense that the goal guides the wanderer's will. The gift of existence, through which the things exist and subsist in their substantial form, is an act of God. If the God-given existence inherent in things is their inner-most essential aspect which grounds, sustains and guides them to-wards their goal and, in so doing, defines their essence through and through, then God is also in all things, and innermostly, by his essence, his presence and power (S. th. I q. 8 a. 1).

God is not only an external and prior foundation—especially for the creature endowed with intellect. It is in its nature always to have him within itself as the goal of its epistemological and voli-tional activity.

The substantial form as the primary act granted to man as his own comes to fruition only through man's promising activity. Since, as a person, man in his intellectual and free nature subsists in a form which lends him existence, his own creaturely causality suits him (cf. the system of *causae secundae*). In the universal and transcendent causality of creation God brings forth the created, in-dependent causes so that, as a result, first, between God and the world, a historical dimension of reality (with the drama of clashing freedoms) originates.

According to Thomas, God is the exemplary cause of all things (*causa exemplaris*). The existence of things is the first inclusive all-determining and always present God's imprint. But an imprint that bears the mark of its cause. That is why the world reflects its founding in the universal wisdom of God, in his thinking and in the freedom of his action. The reasonable structure of things, their perfection in their substantial form is grounded in an exemplary manner in the mind and in God's ideas. Of course, the multiplicity of worldly things does not cancel God's simplicity. Without their realization in creation they merge in the Logos with God's self-knowledge. Their multiplicity in the context of creation results from the different levels of participation of beings in existence and, hence, in God's mind or self-knowledge.

Unlike man, however, God does not come to the intellectual forms and ideas of things through discursive thinking. He knows the world through his own essence in which he always knows himself. Not because there is multifold existence from God does he know it, but because he thinks, makes it into the additional object of his knowledge, does it exist at all in its finite realization.

The statement that the world has always been co-existent as a potentiality in God's idea must not be interpreted in the sense of a passive potency (as, for example, in the case of matter). It means God's active potency through which God in his infinite self-knowledge, at the same time, also creates all the finite realities in the same moment in which he knows them, or knows by creating them.

Furthermore, God is the final cause (*causa finalis*) of all creation. If creatureliness means more than the mere fact of existence, if it instead expresses the inner relationship of all things created to God, then God is revealed rightly in creatures as their transcendent goal. God, however does not make himself a goal in order to achieve something for himself. He is pure self-realization beyond the creaturely alternation between rest and activity (*agens tantum*). In his creative activity God wants to communicate his perfection, which is identical with his goodness (S. th. I q. 44 a. 4). With his creative activity he communicates the participation made possible by grace

in the fulfillment of his being through which he is always identical
with himself in his self-knowledge and in his loving will to self-hood.
If man in his knowledge and his action that aims at unification in
love, embraces himself, then he embraces himself in his orientation
towards his goal, God, and in his participation in divine knowledge
and divine love. For this reason, mediated through grace, the co-accomplishment of divine knowledge and divine love, through which
God is identical with himself, is the perfection of man's intellectual
and volitional activity and, hence, of his creatureliness generally.

## The immediacy of God's creative activity and the uniqueness of God as Creator

The Christian concept of God can only be maintained if it can be
shown in the cross-check that the world (including the materia prima
or *quantitate signata*) proceeds from nothing, if, therefore, God is the
sole and absolute ontological foundation of the world in its existence,
in the concrete individual beings, in the orders and in all immanent
particular causalities. Because God's being is impartible, he cannot
impart his creative activity to other creatures (contrary to Avicenna
and Peter Lombard). This results in a basic definition of the creation
and a precise formulation of the Christian understanding of God:

> [Creation is] the emanation of all being from the univer-
> sal cause, which is God; and this emanation we desig-
> nate by the name of creation. (S. th. I q. 45 a. 1)

> Creation is the production of a thing in its entire sub-
> stance, nothing being presupposed either uncreated or
> created. Hence it remains that nothing [and nobody] can
> create except God alone, who is the first cause. (ibid. q.
> 65 a. 3)

## The incomparability of God in relation to the world

The concept creation designates the ontologically founded primal
relationship between God and the world. But if God's relation to the

world meant the same as the world's relation to God as its Creator, the consequence would be God's finitude. The creational relationship between God and the world is not integral to God's essence but is freely established (*relatio rationis*). In it is revealed only the essential nature of the world's relation to God. For the creature it is a real relation (*relatio realis*) that bestows essence. For God it is the free act of his gracious love. Creatureliness, therefore, is in reality realized in creation, while, when viewed from God's perspective, it is grounded in the freedom of bringing forth the world and its orientation towards God as its origin and goal of its movement (S. th. I q. 45 a. 3)

### The threefold God as the origin and goal of creation

In compliance with the doctrine of the Lateran Synod of 649 (DH 501) and the Lateranense IV (DH 800), Thomas also says that no one Divine Person apart from the others is the sole Creator of the world. The one God brings forth the creation in the unity of his nature and in the trinity of the persons. Thomas adds that God's creative activity occurs corresponding to the inner order of the egresses of the divine persons. For if the world must be seen as God's work then a certain correspondence with God as its universal foundation of its existence is reflected in it.

However, as we can see from the revelation, God is the Father who knows himself in the act of bringing forth the Son and with him in the Holy Spirit loves himself as God. The Father as Creator brings forth the world, the Son brings it forth as Creator through his Word and as the archetype of all created things, and the Holy Spirit brings forth the world in its intrinsic orientation towards participation in the love of the divine persons.

Hence, the revelation of the Trinity is vital to think correctly about creation (defending against the doctrine of God's poverty and to emphasize that the creation was the mediation of pure love and goodness and not motivated by necessity) and, in addition, to think correctly about the salvation of humanity, which is "accomplished by the Incarnate Son, and by the gift of the Holy Spirit" (S. th. I q. 32 a. 1 ad 3).

In creatures of less spirituality there are merely weak traces of the creative activity of the threefold God. For man it is the subsistent form of his soul along with knowledge and freedom which represents a likeness of the threefold God in the manner of an image. In its dimensions the soul represents God's trinitarian creative activity and, hence, the soul is also disposed for the encounter with the self-revelation of the threefold God in salvation history.

God himself is the One that knows himself in his Word, Son, and lovingly possesses himself as the Holy Spirit. Man, the highest form of participation in existence in the dimensions of the One, True and Good, is, as a person, himself indivisibly one who knows himself in his inner word and, hence, is given mind and freedom (without these accomplishments being personally formative as in God). His intellectual being is the source of all worldly knowledge and—mediated by it—the knowledge of God as well as the volitional orientation towards him. The identity of the will with the goodness that God himself achieved in action is called love. The human soul receives through the historical self-mediation of the Father, his Word and the Holy Spirit, a *similitudo trinitatis*. It is disposed to an active participation in the trinitarian life of divine love (to the perception of the one and threefold God, as he is: Council of Florence, Decree *Laetentur caeli*: DH 1305).

### The order of the world as an expression of God's goodness

The world can only reflect God's unity in the multiplicity of creatures. The polymorphous order of the world of the physical and biological plurality of things, of living things and their levels from lifeforms with personalities to single-celled creatures is a metaphor of God's inexhaustible creative power and goodness. Hence, the world produced is not a chaos but, as a whole and in detail, a positive expression of God's comprehensive ordering power.

Hence, viewed anthropologically, the distinction made between the sexes is also a reminder of God's comprehensive will to order through which he communicates his goodness.

Even if Thomas also adopts the biological and sociological un-
derestimation of the female sex from the natural scientific views of
the day, he still says, on the anthropological and grace-theological
level, that human existence as male and female, the personhood of
the female, her quality of being made in God's likeness and of being called to participate in eternal life corresponds to the creative
will of God, fully in correspondence with the *universalis auctor
naturae* (cf. S. th. I q. 92 a. 1 ad 1).

## If God, where does evil come from?

If God is the Author of everything that exists in the world, must
he then also be the Author of the difference between good and evil?

Similar to St. Augustine, Thomas also excludes the existence of
evil as a substance created by God (cf. the whole thematic *quaestio
disputata de malo*).

If creation is not simply some casual generation of an existence
of some kind or other but rather a representation of the being, wisdom and goodness of God vitalized by the granting of participation bestowed upon God's first and most original likeness (De ver.
q. 22 a. 2 ad 2), the concept of a created, evil substance proves to be
a contradiction in itself.

We must examine in what sense *malum* first arises as a theological problem.

It is not problematic that the creation involves mortality in general and, hence, the corruptibility of individual beings. It is intrinsic to finite being that it can also violate or serve as sustenance for
others (e.g., in respect to predators and their prey; the killing of
animals for human sustenance).

The actual meaning of *malum* is also inappropriate if a living
thing is not perfect, if it is missing something which is not intrinsic
to its nature (e.g., that a horse cannot speak).

Worthy of theological consideration is not the *malum privative
dictum* but rather the *malum negative dictum* (i.e., that a being is
missing something that is in fact an intrinsic part of its form; e.g.,
that someone as a result of an accident can no longer speak), i.e.,

the purposeful negation of the good. A distinction must also be drawn between the particular corruptibility attendant to the finiteness of the creation (such as corporeal and psychic injuries to man) or the total corruption of the body (in death), on the one hand, and the morally evil on the other.

The real question pertains to *malum morale*: How can a created good will, or a created freedom, willingly bring forth evil?

Creation means that God by virtue of the *causa efficiens transcendentalis* brings forth the creature by means of the form characteristic in substance of his being and, by so doing, consummates it as well.

The form as the substantiating act and self-realization, however, is understood in a dual sense: as *actus primus*, to the extent that God endowed man in the first place with an intellectually gifted nature which is consummated in its free will and specifically in this way lets man find fulfillment in his form; but mention should also be made of an *actus secundus*, to the extent that this form can only be consummated by the immanent self-action bestowed on it to move towards the goal outside of itself (*operatio ad finem*). Based on this self-action of the substantial form of man (*actus* or *liberum arbitrium*) the moral evil can originate if the human will falls short of his natural goal, goodness and God as the Author of Goodness and the final cause of man's self-transcendence.

Moral evil, therefore, does not consist in the absence of a substantial form but is a shortage of *actus secundus*, to the extent that this can only be accomplished by his action towards (reaching) goodness.

The truly evil does not exist materialiter because damage has been done to something good. Formally, the morally evil consists in how a created, and hence substantially good will, in its self-realization, turns its back on the naturally intrinsic goal (*malum morale negativum*).

But if God is the Creator of the will, is not a certain share of the blame his? Certainly, God created the substantial *forma voluntatis* and its intrinsic *operatio liberi arbitrii in finem boni*. In respect to man's spiritual and free nature, God is the transcendental foundation and the empowerment of its realization. But God is not the substantial form, not the formal and material foundation through which man directly fulfills himself in his freedom and decision of conscience. God is the Creator of human freedom. But since man exists through the being bestowed upon him, the fulfillment of his will is a direct realization of himself. Man is the lord of his own deeds. By being mediated to himself and by subsisting directly from the being bestowed upon him as his own, his execution of his will is neither an appearance of the divine volitional act nor the mechanical effect of a quasi physical cause of divine influence which he could not escape from.

That is why man is himself directly the author of his own movement towards goodness as his transcendent goal. For this reason, on the other hand, he himself is also directly responsible if he withdraws from the natural dynamic process of moving towards goodness. Hence, God is never the Author of evil in the moral sense, i.e., in the sense of blame.

Naturally, no evil in substance is created by the deficient movement of man's will. The human will cannot bring forth any *per se malum,* and posit it as its goal, that does not at all exist in itself. It can only set this goal *per accidens.* That is why moral evil exists in the will itself as its perversion and as its self-destruction (*privatio boni*). Moral evil is the injustice of a criminal act, not the damage which it inflicts on its victim.

Even though God can never be seen as the Author of moral evil in terms of blame, he is the Author of the punishment for moral evil. In the punishment, however, God does not impose an extrinsic sanction that is heterogeneous in respect to the circumstances or the act. Punishment designates only the inner consequence of the actively free will whose naturally intrinsic goal in goodness is negated. Hence, the punishment is nothing other than the corresponding wages of the evil deed (cf. Rom 6:23: "For the wages of sin is death," because the sin distracts man from his goal to the extent that God is man's life). Hence, God is the Author of misfortune to the extent that it originates as the consequence of sin (*auctor poenae*), for: God arranged the world such that a confused mind becomes a punishment unto itself.

In the punishment God also reveals the order of his righteousness. God's righteousness is nothing other than his communication of his goodness, which appears in the order of the world. God's righteousness towards the sinner (biblically expressed: "wrath," "vengeance"; e.g., Nah 1:2 f.) is nothing other than the revelation of his zealous love. In this moment, God encounters the sinner as Author from whom the human self-transcendence of the free will has strayed and the perfection of everything good and the salvation withdrawn from the sinner. God as the Author of the "punishment for sin" grants in the "punishment" the grace of repentance of the heart and the turning of the will to the direction of his own essential perfection in goodness. This is nothing other than the joy of the loving unity with God. To the victim of an evil deed (or a natural catastrophe or a historical tragedy) God reveals himself not as an avenger of the victim's own, earlier evil deeds (by which he would turn the criminal into the agent of his righteousness and vengeance), but as the saving and healing God who overcomes death, mourning, wailing and pain forever (Rev 21:4).

## d) Developments in the Late Middle Ages

The theology of creation certainly reached a high point in the works of Bonaventura and Thomas Aquinas, but by no means its end. Having completely accepted the creation doctrine, other theologians, reverting to other philosophical-theological traditions and, in light of new challenges, interpreted the belief in creation in part in a new theological conception. Not consciously departing from Thomas, but rather in contradiction to an assertion of the independence of knowledge in relation to faith, and even to the emphasis on the possibility of philosophical truths that deviate from theological knowledge of truth (in Averroistic Arestotelism), John Duns Scotus (approx. 1265–1308) emphasizes that individual aspects of

the belief in divine creation can only be completely illuminated
reasonably by turning to revelation. Although he also believes in
the philosophical provability of creatio ex nihilo (Op. Ox. II d.1
q. 2 n. 3, 4), but not that God can be shown by evidence to be the
clear omnipotent cause of the world. The essential presence in the
created things must also be attributed more to belief than to philosophical argumentation (Rep. Paris. I d. 37 q. 2 n. 10).

To be able to prove God's existence philosophically, Duns Scotus must establish a univocal concept of being. Only if being, as
the first object of the intellect, encompasses everything knowable
in the term, can this term, obtained in this way, be attributed to
all being, both the divine and creaturely? However, this occurs in
the modal difference of infinite and finite, whereby being is not
a genus term that encompasses God and the creature and, hence,
would categorize God himself and, finally, subordinate him to
creaturely reason (cf. Ord. I d. 8 q. 3 n. 16).

The essence of the act of creation, however, does not consist in
how God alone causally brings forth finite being, allowing participation in being (in the sense of the doctrine of analogy of Thomas),
but that he brings it forth in a unique way. For Scotus, too, the
world exists ideally in God's intellect. But God does not bring
forth the various things of creation simply by thinking them. The
contingency of the world originates in a willful (volitional) jointure
of the primal ideas of simple things in the divine intellect and the
complex ideas of things composed of form and matter. The reality created is not primarily an indication of the divine intellect.
Instead, its contingency points to how God constitutes it, through
the freedom of his will to act. In this way, God reveals himself
first and foremost as a free will in relation to the world. This act
of jointure is born by God's will that is naturally a reasonable loving will. In relation to God, the world proves to be dependent on
his will through and through (*dependentia essentialis*; voluntarism).
The will of creation is in a certain manner itself contingent and no
longer identical with God's essence (apart from the created world).
Hence, for Scotus, it is very important to emphasize freedom in

relation to the creation and to underscore the inner contingency of the created world.

In the context of nominalism of the Late Middle Ages, William of Ockham (1285–1349) expresses increased doubt in the philosophical and, hence, logical provability of the evincibility of divine creation. The link between God and the creation is not grounded in the primal ideas of the divine intellect such that God's general ideas appear in the forms of the created things. The general terms developed by human reason are not the compilation which reflects God's reason as it is expressed in the creation (*universalia in re*), they are only the schemes of classification of our subjective reason based on the composition of the physical form and matter (*universalia post rem*). Creatures exist in their individuality and not in a generalizable singularity. Hence, they are known by God as his free dispositive acts. They exist without God having also revealed his essence in his acts (cf. I Sent. d. 35,9,5; Ord. d. 35 q. 2). The being of things does not include access to God by way of reason. The only band joining them to God is the free will of his omnipotence. Contingency no longer means the inner positivity based on participation in being and, hence, God's knowability due to his in-existence *per essentiam* in the world. The omnipotence of God's will (*potentia Dei absoluta*) finds its "limit" in the logical law of contradiction (Quodl. 6, 1). Of course, the world is orientated by the positively and contingently realized will of God towards him in its physical state and in life of grace (*potentia Dei ordinata*).

Even if this position has absolutely nothing to do with the distorted image of "God's arbitrariness in nominalism," still, here, the theology of revelation and philosophical theology, belief and reason, a theological view of the God-world relationship and a philosophical or natural scientific view of the empirically comprehensible world clearly go their separate ways. By allowing the scholastic metaphysics, orientated towards the forms of essence and ideas, to retreat, Ockham has also become the initiator of modern natural science, that limits itself to concrete, empirical, quantitative and experimentally provable facts (the single, individual factors).

Hence, this is also connected to how a philosophy that builds on experience (i.e., on the quantitative-sensual and not on the experience of the essentiality of things acquired through abstraction) was no longer capable of presenting belief in God the Creator as reasonable. With a concept of reason so narrowly restricted to the world of experience, those in natural theology within the framework of a mechanistic worldview could at best only conclude the existence of an absolutely intelligent divine master craftsman. The Christian view of God as one who reveals himself in the creation and as person-reality mediating salvation could, hence, only be put forward in a purely positive way based on the authority of the historical revelation testimonies, but no longer be opened to insight based on reason.

A theological instrumentalization of the new cosmology in connection with the emerging natural science was attempted on the basis of a neo-Platonic exemplarism by Nicolaus Cusanus (1401–1464). He comprehends God as an absolute unity. In the sense of his fundamental doctrine of the coincidence of opposites (*coincidentia oppositorum*), God, as the absolute maximum, also comprises its opposite, the absolute minimum, and is expressed in it and through it. On the basis of the essential difference between infinite being of the Creator and the contingency of the world, the absolute unity and greatness of God is made explicit in the creaturely diversity of the finite (*explicatio*). By contrast, the diversity of the finite finds its ideal unity in God (*complicatio*). God is creatively active life that manifests itself in finiteness in many ways. In this way, Cusanus can take up the new worldview with the idea of the infinite world as endless space and unlimitable time (relation and inner mirroring of macrocosmos and microcosmos). In this way, the world of created eternity in the representation of the greatest and the smallest becomes a created image of the eternity and unity of God in its living activity and distinctiveness, as it is essentially present in God's triunity (*De docta ignorantia* II, 7). Cusanus's description of the world as a "created God" and man as "a God appearing in man" clearly approaches the late medieval criticism of the ontological thinking of the scholastics, the emerging worldview of the natural sciences and the optimistic self-image of man in Renaissance philosophy (cf. Giovanni Pico della Merandola, *De dignitate hominis*, 1486).

---

Who could understand the following?: how all things are the image of that one, infinite Form and are different contingently—as if a created thing were a god manqué... For the Infinite Form is received only finitely, so that every created thing is, as it were, a finite infinity or a created god, so that it exists in the way in which this can best occur. (*De docta ignorantia* II, 2)

---

Cusanus's creation theology, neo-Platonically influenced, should nevertheless not be understood as pantheistic as the theology of Giordano Bruno (1548–1600) or, in the dialectical sense, as in the case of Hegel (1770–1831). There are clearly tangible connecting lines to the neo-Platonically colored Christian mysticism of Meister Eckhart (1260–1327/28; cf. also the condemnation of ambiguous sentences: DH 951–53; 976 f.) and later regarding Jakob Böhme (1575–1624), regarding Franz von Baader (1765–1841) as well as the most important representatives of German idealism (Fichte, Schelling).

## 4. In the Context of the New Worldview of the Natural Sciences and the Foundational Crisis of Metaphysics and Philosophical Theology

### a) General Context

Christian theology maintains, in the creation teaching in particular, its basic understanding of reality and the universal claim to validity of faith. Because "it is... evident that the opinion is false of those who asserted that it made no difference to the truth of

the faith what anyone holds about creatures, so long as one thinks
rightly about God... For error concerning creatures engenders a
false science of God" (Thomas v. A., S. c. g. II c. 3). After prov-
ing the rationality of Christian faith and asserting the possibility
of theology as a science, the central task in the re-orientation of
European thinking in "the modern era" consisted in grappling
with the (and historical) worldview of natural science (primarily with Copernicus, Galileo Galilei, Kepler, Newton and, in the
nineteenth century, primarily with Charles Darwin's theory of
biological descent). In these instances it was not really the substantially expanded knowledge about the structure and effectiveness
of empirically understandable nature but the epistemologically
critical and ontological implementation in philosophy that, on
the basis of the new worldview, was enquiring into the possibility
of metaphysics, including a philosophical theology: in rationalism (Descartes, Spinoza, Leibniz, Wolff), criticism (Kant) and
idealism (Fichte, Schelling, Hegel). Hence, skepticism, agnosticism and anti-metaphysical conceptions of empiricism (primarily
Locke, Hume) and the materialists of the eighteenth and nineteenth centuries (Lamettrie, Condillac, Helvetius, Holbach; D.F.
Strauß, A. Ruge, M. Stirner, Feuerbach, Marx, Nietzsche, Freud),
which were combined with Darwinism into monistic Weltan-
schauung doctrines ("Everything is undifferentiated matter") (e.g.,
Ernst Haeckel, *Welträtsel,* 1899).

The efforts of modern philosophy to account for the basic statements of Christian dogma in terms of philosophical reason did not
arise at all from a conscious renunciation of metaphysics and the
theology of the Middle Ages. Nor, by any measure, can the overall
development be understood as human reason's process of emancipation from heterogeneous metaphysical and theological claims,
at whose absolute end, as the ultimate result of the human history
of ideas, a naturalistic immanentism and atheism must stand that
alone can be justified in the light of critical reason.

In truth, modern subjective philosophy is a new conception of
reality and human reason in the light of new methods and the

substantial knowledge of the natural sciences prepared by developments of late medieval philosophy (nominalism, neo-Platonic mysticism). The point was to overcome the separation of nature and mind, the singular and the general, of sensual experience and transcendental reflection, of the sensually grasped individual object and the supra-individual, general idea, for theology based on supernatural revelation and a philosophical-metaphysical theology that was based solely on reason.

## b) The Physico-Theology as an Answer to the New Physics

The new, experimental science no longer viewed nature in terms of philosophical abstraction of the form of essence (the invisible reality-bestowing substance) and, finally, in the horizon of being. The object is the immediately tangible thing in its sensually perceptible, quantifiable and measurable characteristics as can be stated in the laws of mechanics, in interaction with other things. The originally philosophical term of substance becomes the epitome of the functional nexus of mechanically describable phenomena and is better described as "system and structure."

Hence, metaphysics in the classical sense no longer can provide a reference point for the Christian belief in divine creation. Instead, it is the enquiry into the founder and sustainer of the world order that is moved by purely mechanical causes. According to the deism originating in England, God has a similar relation to the world in an outward sense as a mechanic to his work (a watchmaker-God): Moreover, the determinable purposefulness of the natural order and its wonderful parallelism with human needs is an indication of God's superior intelligence. Hence, this physico-theology can refer to God's revelation in the "book of nature" (cf. as early as in the School of Chartres in the Early Middle Ages). Furthermore, the search for an empirical verification of the teleological principle is characteristic.

The disadvantage of such a postulate of God as a kind of "working hypothesis" was, for one, that God could no longer act historically contingently in the world (suspicions regarding "interventionism"; doubts regarding miracles and salvation history), and, for another, that, with the expansion of knowledge about immanent causes, God could become superfluous as a working hypothesis (Laplace as quoted by Stephen Hawking).

### c) The Philosophical Tendency Towards Naturalism

However, where the possibilities and limits of the new experience-based science are no longer seen from the perspective of the consciously set methodical reduction but rather where the material structure grasped under these conditions becomes the standard and the limit of all human knowledge of reality, concept formation and the final horizon of truth, what originates is a rationalistic and monistic naturalism that expressed itself in philosophical systems (empiricism, sensualism, materialism, logical positivism, critical rationalism). All of these share the tension between the immeasurable expansion of human knowledge in the area of empirical registration of the world and the domination of the world, on the one hand, and an extreme reduction in the human potential for knowledge in fields of metaphysics or even theology.

Since human reason is no longer capable of attaining to knowledge of the mental forms of things and their supra-individual ideas rooted in God's intellect but rather only to sensual perception, David Hume (1711–1776) can trace the basic categories of previous metaphysics, namely substance and the metaphysical principle of causality as well as the substantiality of the soul to a purely sensual-psychologically conditioned and, hence, to an a posteriori origin. God, the soul, immortality, the world as a whole in its transcendental relation to its Author are not the objects and real conditions of thinking but merely the individual or collective psychologically conditioned sensual configurations or illusions.

Paradigmatic for the overall tendency towards empirical naturalism is Paul Henri Thiry d'Holbach (1721–1789), who in his work *Système de la nature*, which appeared in 1770, traces back all phenomena to matter which has been eternally existent. It is only through mechanical (biological and chemical) laws that matter takes on its forms. It is formed in man, in the higher-life forms and in consciousness. According to Lamettrie (1709–1751), man is only a complex natural structure, highly organized matter, a machine. Hence, the ideal contents of his consciousness, such as primarily the idea of God and the moral laws, are products of sensuality. This can be interpreted in terms of developmental psychology (as pertinent to the "childhood stage" of humanity) or in terms of social policy (as instruments of the church or priestly deception) (cf. also, following the same pattern, the developed exposure theories: L. Feuerbach, *Wesen des Christentums*, 1841: Werke V, hg. v. E. Thies, F 1976, 95–142; K. Marx, *Nationalökonomie und Philosophie*, 1844: *Frühschriften*, hg. v. S. Landshut, St 1964, 246–248; S. Freud, *Die Zukunft einer Illusion*, W 1927.

Postulatory atheism was also frequently legitimated by a criticism of creation dogma.

Ernst Bloch (1885–1977) opposes the *Deus creator* with the *Deus spes* (*Atheismus im Christentum. Zur Religion des Exodus und des Reichs*, F 1968, 63 f.) He understands the God of creation as a legitimation of the existing and the dominant structures of injustice. If, as stated in Gen 1:31, everything made by God is good, then there is nothing left for man to accomplish, and he has been stripped of his critical potential to bring about change and to constitute his freedom autonomously.

In the positivistic philosophy and in critical rationalism the metaphysical enquiries into being and the theological enquiry into God and man's relation to transcendence are considered as meaningless and pointless (R. Carnap, *Die Überwindung der Metaphysik durch logische Analyse der Sprache: Erkenntnis* 2, 1931, 219–241; H. Albert, *Das Elend der Theologie*, 1979). This transcendence-less sense of time of a monistic naturalism finds its validity in the message of human life and life in general as "merely a flash in the pan, . . . a stage in the decay of the solar system" (B. Russel, *Why I am not a Christian; Warum ich kein Christ bin*, M 1963, 24).

The reference to the modern contributions to knowledge in astrophysics and evolutionary research merely appears to enable human thought to return to the cosmocentricity of antiquity with its pathos over transience, when Jacques Monod states: "L'ancienne alliance est rompue; l'homme sait enfin qu'il est seul dans l'immensité indifférente de l'Univers d'où il a émergé par hasard." (*Le hasard et la nécessité*, 1970, 224; *Zufall und Notwendigkeit*, M 31971, 219)

## d) The Subjective-Philosophical Reconstitution of Metaphysics and Philosophical Theology

René Descartes (1596–1650) wants to save the independence of the cognitive-ideal reality. For the empirical world there was no longer any certain point of departure whatever to access the contents of philosophy and theology. Of course, he does not start from the experience of the individual being and the abstraction of its forms of essence, as in ontology, in order to arrive in his concluding step at the ideas of divine intelligence.

By attaining to the unshakable foundation of every philosophical reflection in consciousness he certainly also overcomes the naive objectivism and the subjective amnesia of a science that thinks it is able to objectively describe reality by excluding any a priori moment which conditions the knowledge of the knowing subject. For Descartes, from the analysis of the finite self-consciousness the idea of God emerges as a necessity that, simultaneously, is the basis for a conclusion of his existence as the point of reference of finite subjectivity. God, the infinite substance, proves to be the Author both of finite substances of the mind (*res cogitans*) and the body (*res extensa*). He also correlates these two substances.

Starting from this, the theological rationalism of the philosophy of the enlightenment drew the conclusion that all the contents of the Christian doctrine had to be deducible based on a priori reason, so that the events in the contingent world of nature and history could not produce anything essentially new. This, in turn, resulted in the major theological problem of correlating dogma and history.

In the further development of the philosophy of consciousness the question arose, how God and the world can be more inwardly re-correlated to one another. In physico-theology, God is only related to the world outwardly. In rational metaphysics (due to the univocalization and the misconceptualization of being) God was understood as the possible concept for a "supreme being." Since the world in its being was, internally, no longer open to God and God, by means of the analogy of the individual being, no longer mediated the hypostatized mystery as the origin and future of man, God seemed to be like a material object somewhere beyond the visible world. However, if, as Kant says, human reason is limited merely to the knowledge of sensually given objects, and it, by dint of its a priori forms, constitutes a concrete phenomenon, then God can only be predicated as an ideal of reason while the question of his real existence cannot be answered. Seen in this way, the proof of an existence of God as a Creator of the world proves to be impossible (KrV B 655).

In order to avoid an objectivistic concept of God, i.e., the idea of God as an essence beyond experience and, finally, dependent on human imagination, Baruch Spinoza (1632–1677) and then German idealism already attempted to develop a more pantheisticizing unity of God and the world, of divine self-unfolding in nature and in human thought as a moment in this process.

Following up on the new definition of substance in Descartes, which states that substance is something which requires nothing else for its own existence (in contrast with the scholastics: Substance is something that does not exist in another), Spinoza concludes that God, as the infinite subsistence, is the sole necessary existence and is the cause of itself (*causa sui*). God or nature (*deus sive natura*) is the all-encompassing reality that unfolds in the modi and accidents of its phenomena in the cognitive and corporeal world. The divine nature and its manifestations interact as process (*natura naturans*) and product (*natura naturata*). Everything that exists is God, and God acts in the process of his self-manifestation in the world only in relation to himself.

The thought of a person standing free in relation to the world (God's reality) and a creation of the world from nothings proves to be senseless and contradictory.

Similar criticism comes from Johann Gottlieb Fichte regarding the use of the concept of a personal God. What arises from this is the strict denial of a creation:

> The assumption of a creation, as the essentially funda-
> mental error of all false Metaphysics and Religion, and,
> in particular, as the fundamental principle of Judaism
> and Heathenism, originates from ignorance of the doc-
> trine which we previously laid down. Compelled to
> recognize the absolute unity and immutableness of the
> divine essence in itself, and being unwilling to give up
> the independent and real existence of finite things, they
> made the latter proceed from the former by an act of
> absolute arbitrariness: which, firstly, utterly destroyed
> their fundamental conception of the godhead and at-
> tributed to it arbitrariness which ran through their
> whole religious system; and, secondly, reason was for
> ever perverted and thought transformed into dreamy
> fantasizing;—for such a creation is impossible to con-
> ceive properly by thought—that is by what can be prop-
> erly called thought—and no man ever did so conceive
> of it. In particular, in relation to religious doctrine, the
> supposition of a creation is the first criterion of the false-
> hood, and the denial of such a creation, should it have
> been set up by any previous system, is the first criterion
> of the truth of such a religious doctrine. (Fichte, Werke
> V, B 1971, 479; *The Way Towards the Blessed Life or, The
> Doctrine of Religion,* tr. by W. Smith, 1849)

The Hegelian philosophy of mind finds itself confronted with a similar problem. God does not relate to the world in terms of a personal freedom that sovereignly calls the world into existence. In a dialectical process of self-differentiation, self-revealing and knowing through the moments of nature, of history and subjective mind, he brings forth the world to himself in his own ordered fullness.

Hegel can show the reasonableness of all dogma in response to the enlightenment to the extent that they represent the self-manifestation of the mind. But in relation to the Christian profession of faith the question remains open of the ontological difference of the world from God, the personhood and the free personal self-relationship of God to the world in the sense of the total cause of its being and its orientation towards God.

## 5. The More Recent Catholic and Reform Controversy over Philosophical Theology as a Portal to Historical Revelation

Against the background of the controversy between Karl Barth and Erich Przywara over the analogy of being and existence as a prerequisite of the theology of knowledge of a supernatural revelation and the inner-protestant controversy over a *Reference Point of the Revelation* (E. Brunner, P. Althaus, W. Joest, W. Pannenberg u.a.) Eberhard Jüngel disputed the necessity and the right of a metaphysical philosophical theology as a prerequisite of God's revelation knowledge (*praeambula fidei*) (*Gott als Geheimnis der Welt. Zur Begründung der Theologie des Gekreuzigten im Streit zwischen Theismus und Atheismus*, Tü 51986).

In the tradition of Reformed theology, Jüngel questions whether the Absolute of philosophical theology, that thinks it can attain to the reason spoiled by the original sin, could have anything at all to do with the God of the revelation and whether it is not more a phantom of God empowering reason. A knowledge of God building on the *Analogia entis* by means of reason is no second source of revelation. The theism of European metaphysics is no more a necessary prerequisite for the revelation and its knowledge than its twin brother, European atheism. God, apparently, only becomes in his self-testimony, in his free Word in history. In the Word, God identifies himself with the Crucified. For this reason there is no other access to God's being prior to and beyond the world through an ahistorical-abstract thinking in the sense that the history of Jesus comes along merely as an accidental modification and supplement to a philosophically conceived God. God can only be experienced in his free self-determination through history, becoming, suffering and the cross. God only arises in human knowledge in which he negates the atheistic negation of God's empowerment. The end of the metaphysical God, i.e., the death of God in philosophy (according to the "speculative Good Friday" in Hegel, *Phänomenologie des Geistes*, 1807) is the prerequisite for a new revelation of the true God in faith alone, namely, faith in God's revelation in the message of the cross.

Hence, creation does not supply a basis for a philosophical theology. It does not prepare an openness for the God of history. The concept of creation must be subsumed exclusively within the crucifixion event. Outside of this staurocentrically interpreted revelation, a belief in God as the Creator of heaven and earth is impossible.

In this way, Jüngel believes that he has already overcome the substantial-objectively conceived God over the world, already criticized in idealism, as a metaphysical prerequisite for the revelation. Simultaneously, the Christian belief in God has become incontestable by atheism and remains untouched by the collapse of philosophical theology, the Christian belief in God has thus become indisputable. Similarly, the opposition between the divine being and the worldly contingent becoming (i.e., the ideal essential truths and the singularity of the contingent) has been overcome. Specifically, God wants to be known through his becoming in history, not in his timeless aseity. Only through his free self-determination in the process of history is he known in his divinity. Since God is freely identified with the Crucified, God is only revealed as the historical God in Jesus Christ (cf. *Gottes Sein ist im Werden*, Tü 31976).

In response to this, Jüngel can be asked, whether self-revelation of God the Creator relevant to salvation already contained in the

Bible, is the encompassing horizon for the historical revelation of God, in which God lets himself be known as the origin and goal of man. It would certainly be wrong if one left Christian belief in divine creation over to the philosophical theologians, to construct a salvifically neutral front and an abstract-faceless understanding of God. But since theology sought out—and must seek out—the discussion with metaphysics and philosophical theology in order to debate belief's universal claim to truth, it cannot merely start with a claim of God's self-revelation in the cross and in the more dialectical contradiction to human reason. It must seek the discussion already in the field of the doctrine of creation and, thus, of the original formulation of its understanding of reality and reason. The purpose of this discourse is not to subordinate belief to reason and the wisdom of the world (cf. 1 Cor 1:21). However, in that theology mediates the Logos of God in the cross to the world, it brings man to the reason of belief. It enables it to realize the personal act of faith in its reasonable self-realization. This is not merely obedience in contradiction to one's own insight but the perfection of created reason and the created will in the participation in God's reason and in contribution to the perfection of his love that he himself is and through which he mediates himself to us. In the cross, God reveals the contradiction to sin, but he also reveals himself as the love that reconciles and hence consummates his creature. The resurrection of Christ from the dead is the revelation of the love of Father, Son and Holy Spirit, that resolves the contradiction of the sin.

# IV

# SYSTEMATIC EXPOSITION

Basic pertinent questions have already been discussed in the preceding historical treatment. This section will review the material from a systematic perspective in the form of a summary. What is meant here by "systematic" is the goal of providing a synthesis of the essential material statements. It would be impossible, however, absolutely to consider God and the world together from the perspective of created reason. The adequate object of our sensually bound, finite reason is the world. While reason can grasp the world, history and man in relation to God and, enlightened by faith through the Holy Spirit, learn to begin to understand God in his acts. But theology can never have God himself in his pure being-in-himself as an object. No created intellect can grasp God as God penetrates and knows himself in his divine Spirit (cf. 1 Cor 2:11f.)

## 1. The Realization of Non-Divine Being through God's Actuality

The discussion about God cannot have its point of departure in his pure existence for himself as if it were possible to ignore the existing world. Reason, creaturely and finite, always starts from experience in the already existent world. The world's being is uncertain to us and the peculiar interlacing of actual experience and its simultaneously accompanying uncertainty of being is what is called created spirit. However, part of the realization of mind is that through the possibility of questioning world experience it sees itself referred to the source of the doubtfulness and the ultimate reason of the world's being, which is inscrutable and which we call God. Hence, a relationship to God is always intrinsic to the constitution of the spirit, especially also to the extent that worldly experience and the doubtfulness of the world belong to it. Whereby, "God" is the designation of the whence of being and spirit. He himself is not a kind of worldly object that is merely also known. Yet man, as spirit, may be fundamentally and constitutively determined by his relatedness to God, who is detached from and unavailable to him. But he must visualize this a priori and transcendental moment of his self-realization a posteriori. In this process God does not become a categorical object. He opens only as the impenetrable horizon towards which we are moving and which we know to be our origin in an absolute sense. The spirit not only transcends itself, however, intentionally towards the infinite. It knows itself, especially in its intentionality, as constituted through the non-worldly absolute of God. Finally, he grasps only through the *reality* of the transcendent God. But, under these conditions, how can man speak of God and his actions?

God is not the world. If God were the world or a piece of the world, then he would not be its absolute foundation, withdrawn from it. God cannot be defined based on the distinctiveness from the world. Nor can the world be the basis on which God comes to himself. But for us the world means possibility of—and the limit to—a discussion about God, and at the same time of coming to the knowledge: God is. This "is" in the judgmental sentence is of course not identical with the being through which God is himself realized.

The world itself is characterized by finiteness. Finiteness means that a single thing only contains reality to a limited degree. Hence, finite intellect can only think of what is finite, namely, what is doubtful and a being which is questionable. However, then, as the real condition of experience and finite being and, simultaneously, doubtfulness, man can form the concept of a being that is pure actuality and that in this does not self-mediate in the mode of doubtfulness. And this is called absolute spirit or pure identity of being and self-knowledge. This term, formed by us, has its basis in the experience of the actuality of the finite world and the finite values that in their existence are dependent on an act of realization beyond their self. The act in which this infinite being is realized, however, is in its self-hood not dependent on us and on our thinking.

We comprehend the concept God as the real condition of our being as spirit in the world and, hence, as the condition of finite reality. In this sense, judgment sentence "God is" is also true; but we do not grasp God in his inner act, through which he is he himself. *We just grasp God only as the mystery as such.*

All the individual beings known to us exist through a realization of general being in the various natures of essence. It exists as concretion of existence and essence. Hence, the essence is the principle of delimiting beings. However, beyond the concrete things, being merges completely with God. It is not through an essentiality through which he would first be mediated by his existence that God is limited, realized and defined. God's being is his essence; God is the pure actuality of his divine being. Due to the unity of being and essence, the "essence" of God, unlike the creature, is not the principle of limited participation.

And in God there is no sequentiality of disposition and its transformation into an action. God does not suddenly emerge out of an eternal repose to act and, hence, bring forth creation. In God's actuality, which is completely identical with him, are the infinite potentialities of finite participation in being. By wanting himself, God can also want something distinct from himself. But it is wanted through a delimiting principle, i.e., a differentiation principle, otherwise it would not be distinctive from God. But existence different from himself is wanted by God. And, for this reason, God is the Author of the world things which are distinct from him in the unity of their existence and form. To the extent that the world only persists in the concretion of existence and essence, it is created by God's Word and will. By existing as finite being distinctive from God, it is created *ex nihilo* and "outside" of God. That does not mean that, at some time, God made room, but rather that the world is realized in its delimited nature and this makes it distinctive from God. God is his own essence through absolute possession of being. World is a reality through a delimiting reception of being as participation in being. The world participates in God's being because through God's will it may exist, specifically in the mode of finiteness, while God exists through himself, in himself, from himself and through his own reality (Eph 4:6).

If God's act of creation coincides outside of created things with God, then it is like unto God: undivided, timeless, immediate reality. God is Creator. He is intimately near to and inwardly present in all created things. He sees the world not only as a whole but in every single thing, no matter when and where it was created, as Creator, up close. So it is by no means so that God was only active as a Creator at the chronological beginning of the universe. He did not at some point in the past leave the world to its own principles of regulation, in order to directly intervene occasionally, now and then, for example, for the sexual conception of man or for some salvific action or another for an individual. Man is not directly related to God because, unlike animals, he was directly created (i.e. outside of the dynamic of the living and the mediation of the sequence of generations), but rather because he was created for immediateness. His spiritual nature is namely the delimiting and concretizing principle of the way of his participation in being. By being directly present and available himself as spirit, the relatedness to the origin of all being whatsoever is also constitutively intrinsic to spiritual being. This relationship with God—even where it does not become thematic—accounts for the subsistence, the prerequisite and condition of what we refer to as personhood.

## 2. Creation Realized through Evolution and the History of Human Freedom

The creative activity of God is the continuous inclusion of the world into God's actuality and its realization through God. But this then also includes that the world, once realized, is also active by means of its immanent principles and that the concrete phenomena in the world can be traced to this activity of immanent principles. Only the human mind has any chance of attaining to the knowledge of its transcendent causes. God has not abandoned his creative activity to the immanent causalities of the world, but rather he effects his reality of creation in the *midst* of the created causes by bearing the world's existence and operation and by granting the world self-empowerment.

Within the most general basic principles of the world there must then be a duality of that which is organized and that which organizes itself: the duality of matter and spirit. Added to this is the coefficient of temporality. The undivided act of creation is effective in the created world only in the manner of evolution.

That, regarding individuals, origin and expiration are general attributes of concrete and finite things cannot be disputed. The key question revolves around whether origin and expiration of genera was integral from the very outset or whether there has been a constancy of the species. If "creation" is God's timeless actuality and presence for created things and not simply identical with what once was at some, somehow chronologically ascertainable beginning of our universe (understood empirically, not metaphysically), then a cognitive advance can be made in this respect.

The fact is that there never is only pure matter. Even what is customarily referred to in the natural sciences as prime matter is not identical with what is meant by materia prima in philosophy. The prime matter which is comprehensible in terms of the natural sciences was also always formed, determined and organized matter. This matter, already somehow organized, i.e., matter formed into a unit of meaning, is in the process of transition to new modalities and singularities.

If natural science refers to matter as inorganic matter, that is legitimate, and at the same time one can treat matter itself solely in terms of quantity, methodologically disregarding its other aspects. But the essence of matter is in this way by no means completely comprehended. The usual way of posing the question always assumes that it is already clear what matter is, while it must be first shown in a complicated argument where there is something called mind in the first place and what mind can be. A more precise analysis of human knowledge and the formation of terms shows that matter is not at all ascertainable. Matter has always been understood by the human intellect *as* matter of an individual being. Hence, the term matter, in itself, is formed by an abstraction from a concretely existing thing, drawn by an abstracting intellect, in the process of knowledge acquisition is impossible to ignore. In reality, therefore, man has always known himself and, in the self-present, matter as the other, through which he is connected to the world, knowing, suffering and acting. At the same time he also needs matter in order to come up to himself. The intellectual immediacy to himself has always been the result of a mediation which courses through the world. At the same time, however, in intellectual realization, the immediate self-givenness is also the prerequisite for the ability of matter to bear a mediation in the first place.

Hence, if there is no knowledge and description of the world without spirit, that does not mean that there could be no world without the human spirit. From his present standpoint, he can easily imagine subpersonal existence, including already before the existence of the human genus. But when he studies pre-human existences, he never comprehends them as pure matter but always as individual material forms marked by structures of meaning. That means, in his intellectual grasp of the world, he identifies the unit of meaning through abstraction and, through the unit of meaning, the world itself. In this perspective he is right to see nature in terms of temporality as a history of matter that organizes itself. In each case, matter is comprehended as individual forms through specific organizational principles. In philosophical terms, one is faced with the being that consists of its essentialities but not absorbed by them. Throughout all of natural history there is a line of development that differentiates being in ever more highly organized forms of meaning. In this way, the fullness of being also presses onwards towards self-transcendence in newly arising

forms. These, so to speak, make up the inner ordering and unifying principle of a more highly arranged matter into an overall
form. On the individual level, this does not exclude but rather
includes a searching interaction of physiological and biological
factors that can also go astray and modify itself in response to
survival chances. The originating life-forms, according to their
species and genus, form themselves as the self-differentiating ves-
sels of being. To the extent that they all originate from the one
being as a continuous flow of life (gene pool), one can see that life
is nothing other than a most sophisticated form of the realization
of being altogether.

As a genus, man then sees himself as the goal of the self-transcendence of being that is organized into a being in the mode of
life and thought.

*With man the natural history of being changes into the history of
ideas.* Nevertheless, the lower forms of self-realization are not absorbed or excluded. Instead, they are integrated into man's intellectual world. That is why, man knows himself in the context of
the whole world of the universe: with its stars and planets, sea and
land, plants and animals.

Man is right to view the world from a human perspective. The
attempt to view the world from a perspective which is not man's
is self-contradictory. The negation of anthropocentricism is itself
only anthropocentricism in a new suit.

In his immediate consciousness man must grasp himself as a consummated intellectual vessel of real being in its essence in which
he subsists as a person. This already includes implicitly the idea of
God. That is why man can also speak of an evolution towards the
more complex. Animal being is more than mere inorganic being.
Thinking is more than a complex kind of organic process. In man,
in the modus of evolution, the self-organizing, created world comes
to itself. Man is the highest form of the realization of the reception
of being, specifically in the mode of being at one with himself.

The timeless act of creation realized in man the created essence
that then can and must make God into its theme, horizon and

the goal of its self-realization. *Beginning with man, natural history is transcended by the history of ideas and the history of freedom.* For man nature is the basis as well as the medium of the self-realization of personified being.

However, in this material-intellectual condition, the self-transcendence of the created person has become possible for the intellectual participation in God's actuality. In other words: The Creator of the world, nature and man, meets man halfway in a personal way as the fulfillment of the self-transcendence of the created spirit. And, here, at the latest, one can see that creation is implicitly God's self-revelation. Creation of finite being and intellect means already in itself the opening of an interminable horizon for God's explicit self-revelation in the WORD. Within it God encounters the created person personally and in the form of a dialog. In the historical revelation in the Word and act of God a divine-human communication history of love, i.e., in SPIRIT, begins.

## 3. God's Self-Revelation as Creator and Redeemer

The one, timeless and indivisible act of creation coincides with God's actuality outside of the created things. However, in his life, God is the purest knowledge of himself. God is infinitely revealed to himself. God is the purest thinking and willing self-disposition. In this sense, God is only known by himself. God's knowledge of himself is identical with God's essence. That is why God alone knows himself adequately in his coessential Word, and God wills himself as loving in his Spirit.

However, to the extent that the infinite actuality of being in created things is realized in a finite manner, created things do not belong adequately to God's awareness of himself; but to the extent that they participate in God's being, they are creaturely media through which we come to the knowledge and the love of God. The knowledge and love of God proves itself in its depth as the creaturely participation in God's self-knowledge and self-affirmation.

Hence the explicit creaturely self-realization of a created mind is nothing other than an event in which God lets himself be known and loved.

We understand the whole of creation as something given in the created things and, in them, God's mediated self-revelation. In that creatures consciously and willingly understand and accept their self-realization as participation in God's self-knowledge and love, God himself is present to them.

As it says in Rom 1:19:

> For what can be known about God is evident to them, because God made it evident to them. Ever since the creation of the world, his invisible attributes of eternal power and divinity have been able to be understood and perceived in what he has made.

Furthermore in Acts 17:27 f.:

> People might seek God, even perhaps grope for him and find him, though indeed he is not far from any one of us. For in him we live and move and have our being.

Furthermore, the church professes in spirit

> one God and Father of all, who is over all and through all and in all. (Eph 4,6)

Hence, God is permanently present through his creative activity in the things created. Every personal intellect is fundamentally destined to participate in the self-revealing being and love of the self-willing God.

Concretely man is never in an abstract facticity of existence but rather always together with the actualization of existence as a dynamic movement towards the perfection in the other. However, once the mere constitutivity (*perfectio formae*) is abstractly lifted from its realization (*operatio in perfectionem finis*), it is called *nature*, but to the extent that this nature is always marked together with its actuality as a movement towards God's presence and the fulfillment through God, we speak of *grace*. If man, in his self-realization as freedom and spirit, turns from God, the result is the loss of grace or guilt (*defectus gratiae*).

The original connection of nature and grace is called creation (*status naturae perfectae per gratiam*). The concrete situation in the unity of nature and grace is called the supralapsarian constitution of man. Of course, the creation cannot be absolutely reversed by sin. The common expression "God withdrew from the creation" is not exact and a mere metaphor. God cannot withdraw at all from creation. It would collapse into nothingness. Therefore it is impossible for God to withdraw from the act of creation because, outside of the created things, it is identical with God. God does not withdraw from creation because of sin; man distances himself from the goodness and beauty of creation in which he exists and in which he knows himself in his dependence on God. In this regard, the created world exists, God is always with it in the present, even if the sinner cannot take on the creation's abundance of grace. In light of the sin, however, the remaining salvific presence of God in his world, in the situation of man's loss of God, takes on the character of redemption. God's creative actuality, through which the creature exists, now reveals itself as forgiveness and reconciliation. *The sinner encounters his Creator in his Redeemer.* But then God's creative activity in the world must also immediately acquire a medium of the redeeming and sanctifying realization. For the sin of man had the effect that the created (especially the intercommunication with his fellow humans in the sacramental character of marriage) was no longer able to be the medium of encounter with God. God's creative activity in the Word that then encounters us in the manner of redemption takes on immediate creaturely reality in Jesus. In Jesus the sinner encounters a creaturely medium completely appropriated by God that mediates him into the immediacy of the Creator, the God of redemption.

Hence, Jesus himself is the perfection, redemption and creative foundation of intellectual nature in its creaturely mediated self-transcendence into the immediacy of God. God's original compassionate actuality in the creation (in his actuality and in the medium of the creaturely realities) is then again accessible, but now concretely as the *grace of Jesus Christ*. In God's incarnated eternal Word and in God's Holy Spirit, poured into hearts, the blessed now have a share in the salvation historically occurring and mediating modus of God's self-revelation and self affirmation. The only way open to God the Creator is through the divine presence in Jesus Christ and the Holy Spirit. In the full sense of the Word, God as Creator is only known through his redeeming activity in Jesus Christ.

## 4. God's Universal World Government and Active Presence in the World

The term of divine world government encompasses the following classical themes of the doctrine of creation: The world's maintenance (*creatio continua*), general and special providence (*providentia*), the predestination of all men to salvation as well as the problematic nature of the relationship of divine and human freedom (*concursus divinus*).

The act of creation comprises within itself, first, a fundamental establishment of the non-divine being and, second, the duration of the act of creation in the created things. Hence, the preservation of the world (*creatio continua*) should not be understood as a type of chronological sequence of individual acts of creation. This concerns the timeless, indivisible presence of the creative actuality in the existence and movement of the world. *God is in/above the world* (Erich Przywara). God's transcendence and imminence are in an inversely proportional relationship to each other. It is only because God is absolutely transcendent in juxtaposition to the world that he can also be immanent in the world in an unsurpassable sense. By being the innermost principle of being and motion for the created realities, he mediates them into their peculiarity and, on the level of their aseity, to their own causality. In classical terminology this is expressed as follows: God is the *causa prima*, that does not cancel the creaturely *causae secundae* (form, matter, causality, finality), but enables it to unfold its own efficacy. God's all-encompassing and constituting creative efficacy and the creaturely immanent causality are neither in a qualitative much less a quantitative continuum of action. Human, spiritual-corporeal reason (at least in principle, if not always factually), in examining the creaturely epistemological object, arrives at a total comprehension of all inner and outer factors that explain the origin, the existence and the expiration of an individual being. However, God, as the transcendent cause, can never be turned to for an explanation of creaturely causalities and functions which have not yet been encompassed. This would be a denial of the perfection of the creation in its inner meaning structure. Moreover, God's transcendent efficient causality would be lowered to the level of created causality. It is not the will of God's transcendent causality to supplement creaturely activities but to empower them to perform their own activities. In its grasp of a creaturely being, creaturely reason encompasses the whole of a thing in the completeness of all the factors that determines its constitution. But reason can also comprehend the whole of a creaturely being in terms of its transcendental relation to the creative act of being in which it is grounded. Hence, the transcendent causality and the categorical causality do not relate to each other like two partial principles that constitute the whole of a thing. Instead, the creaturely causality completely constitutes the whole of a being in the categorical term, while the transcendent causality completely constitutes the whole of a thing according to its being. Only human understanding is in the position to grasp the totality of the world from a dual perspective. God's "intervention" into the world can never mean a suspension of creaturely causality. But God can make creaturely causality into the instrumental courses of his specific salvific will in relation to man. (The acts of creation, the incarnation, the resurrection of the dead have no instrumentally created causality.) After God has brought forth the reality of creation, there is a combined impact of a transcendent cause and the categorical causes without an intermingling and without a separation through which God mediates and empowers the individual beings into their concrete form.

In the discussion about the concrete cooperation of God and man, the limit of the traditional model of language must also be clear. The limit is simply already in the terminology itself. The discussion of cause and effect is taken from the physical-empirical area. But physical causes complement each other in an additive manner or they limit each other reciprocally. If you just transfer this language and thought model to God's action and the deeds of men in freedom without deliberation, you get into unresolvable *aporiae*. These *aporiae* can be attributed to the model of visualization, and do not arise from the matter itself. Because, in this context, seduced by the language, one falls into aporiae, one must not merely talk oneself out of the matter simply by referring to the mystery. However, we must speak in a thoroughly consistent sense, because this connection of God's activity and human activity is, of course, never adequately illuminable. Only God knows in the knowledge of his own essence what he himself is and what the creature is in relation to him. As it is, human beings can only think of the connection between God and man in a creaturely way.

In summary it can be stated: God is the universal cause of human existence. And God also bears and empowers the categorical causes that mediate man into his form and, hence, describe and determine the mode of the reception of being. It is also true that the form of man represents a realization of being in the mode of cognitive being for itself and the free being of the will. What's more, freedom is for man not merely something added to his existence, but freedom is his concrete form of existence. Man does not just have mind and freedom; more to the point, he *is* mind and freedom, although in a finite sense.

# 5. Creation and Grace, Principles of Created Freedom, or the Secret of Providence

Since the transcendent God moves everything in accordance with its created nature, he also moves mankind in accordance with its nature of freedom. Predestination does not mean the sublation of freedom but rather, through the acceptance in faith, the empowerment to make the general salvific will the principle of self-motivation towards the promised goal (cf. Thomas, S. th. I q. 22 a. 1: "In rebus autem invenitur bonum, non solum quantum ad substantiam rerum, sed etiam quantum ad ordinem earum in finem, et praecipue in finem ultimum, qui est bonitas divina. ... Ratio autem ordinandorum in finem proprie providentia est"). This relation between the absolute determination of mankind by God in his self-determination and mankind's spiritual self-motivation, the essence of its freedom, can now be expressed better as follows: God does not exercise any physically measurable influence on created freedom. This would, after all, only limit it, and the effect of the human act of freedom would only be a combination of a divine and a human contribution. In this sense, God would rescind matter's own disposition to act (as *causa secunda*). In reality God exercises his universal influence on the freedom thus created by encountering it as the *motive* of its action. In this context, personal categories must be considered. This is the only exit out of the dead-end embittering discussions which have continued since the seventeenth century.

The Catholic understanding is best expressed by the keyword of God's universal efficacy (instead of exclusive efficacy), that instead of compromising the creature's freedom, empowers it. However, how, with the help of personal categories, can one now describe more precisely the relationship of God's universal causality and the creature's freedom (*concursus divinus*)?

The essence of man is freedom. But we must not describe freedom negatively. Freedom is not realized where I may do whatever is possible for me within the scope of my sensuous demands. Freedom must be seen positively. It describes the possibility of man's perfection in the encounter and in the final unity with the other person. In the process, the man's sensuality must not be left to itself. It must be integrated by him into his personal perfection as the medium of self-transcendence and person encounter with the other person. This inner, reciprocally determining unity of inner will and the lively condition of the human spirit is the ethical form of will. However, intrinsic to every human freedom is a dynamic excess that cannot be fulfilled by another human, who himself is a creature. The human I–you encounter, in particular, does not stand in the way of man's self-transcendence to God, but rather sets it in motion. Finally, due to the source of creaturely freedom in God it can only find its fulfillment in God. Where God himself encounters me even in his freedom in the self-expressing divine Word, he always actualizes the fulfillment of my freedom, hence, of my self. In the positive sense of freedom this offer by God means the fulfillment of my self-transcendence. That is why God, in his freedom, is no limitation for me, but rather first and foremost the removal of limits on the dynamic movement of creaturely freedom in its perfection.

Even in inner-worldly life people have experienced: The human will is dynamically oriented towards a reality which is distinct from him. When he achieves it, i.e., is identified with it and becomes one with it, he is not limited but rather the dynamic reaches its goal. The unity with the loved one is always experienced as the perfection of the love of the lover. In this sense, the lover who sees his love fulfilled in the loved one, always attributes his perfection, his happiness, to the loved one who accepts him and not only his love alone.

Only the gratitude of the joyful can say: "Everything is grace" (Georges Bernanos). Man, to whom God himself has become the motive of his action, his self-design in the world, for this reason, knows himself quasi (biblically worded) as the stuff in the hands of the Creator who forms him. In his profession, therefore, he says that God works in him to desire and to work (Phil 2:13). But, at the same time, he does not see himself incapacitated and cheated of his freedom and his personhood. On the contrary, he feels himself empowered to live out his freedom. Only in the realization of his freedom does he know himself as enabled, through God's self-giving, to act towards the goal. And love in the realization is the only way as it is for the loved one. With him as the motive, it is orientated towards the goal and set into motion. Freedom has its perfection only in the realization towards its goal by which it is also made possible. And the realization moving towards its goal was only made possible by the immediate presence of the goal. In this sense, in the doctrine of grace, Paulus (1 Cor 4:7) is repeatedly quoted: "What do you possess that you have not received?" Particularly in the reception of the new creaturely being, man has become an agent of God and his grace (1 Cor 3:9). In this sense, the activity of freedom is empowered by the presence of grace, to take on the grace towards the goal of self-actualization.

Freedom is enabled by the grace to accept being accepted by God even in one's own realization. In grace God reveals himself as the eternal source of created freedom and its eternal horizon as love:

> For by grace you have been saved through faith, and this is not from you; it is the gift of God; it is not from works, so no one may boast. For we are his handiwork, created in Christ Jesus for the good works that God has prepared in advance, that we should live in them. (Eph 2:8–10)

# THE SELF-REVELATION OF THE THREEFOLD GOD IN THE CONSUMMATION OF MAN

*(Eschatology)*

# I

# HORIZONS AND PERSPECTIVES OF ESCHATOLOGY

## 1. Eschatology and Its Place in Dogmatics

In the manuals of Dogmatics, influenced by neo-Scholasticism, the eschatology (following Sir 7:40 Vg.; Matt 12:45 Vg.) was understood as the doctrine of "last things." Hence, it was also considered to be the final treatise in the dogmatic (*de novissimis*), the one that discussed the themes of *death* and *judgment* (of individual men after their death) as well as *heaven* and *hell* (considered as the two eschatological final conditions following the end of the world and the general judgment).

The label "eschatological" not only serves to classify the realities that follow death "as final." It serves primarily to elucidate the self-revelation of the threefold God expressed in his firm resolve that man be saved. God offers himself eschatologically, i.e., finally and unrepentantly, as the horizon, substance and consummation of human existence, and revealed himself as the origin and goal of man in his transcendental dependence grounded in the creation. In creation and consummation God reveals himself as identical, as "the first and the last" (Isa 41:4), the "one who lives" (Rev 1:18), the "Alpha and Omega . . . , the beginning and the end" (Rev 22:13).

This is why "eschatology" is more than a single theological treatise. It is also an integral structural principle of the revelation and of the response to it, Christian existence. For it is in faith, hope and

love that man—in the here and now—stands unified with God
and, now, already participates definitively in the life of the threefold God. This understanding of the eschatological as an already
present quality of the revelation and man's response in faith, however, does not exclude the future horizon of the final fulfillment
and consummation of the world and man. However, the present
and the future dimension of the eschatology are not outwardly in
juxtaposition to each other. In fact, the presential eschatology is
the dynamic principle through which the believer lets himself be
moved towards his ultimate goal by God.

At the same time, this precludes the misunderstanding that
eschatology--the doctrine of last things--offers, so to speak, a description of the condition of man after his death in an empirically
understood world, or that eschatology is, so to speak, advance information, theologically presented, about the final condition of the
cosmos, described materially and empirically.

Eschatology must be developed strictly in the horizon of God's
self-mediation to man in terms of revelation theology. It finds a
Christocentric apogee in Jesus Christ as the "last man" (ἔσχατος
Ἀδάμ, 1 Cor 15:45 ff.). The faith in God's definitive self-mediation
in his Son and the outpouring of the divine spirit in the "last
days" (Acts 2:17; cf. 1 Cor 15:52; 1 Tim 4:1; 2 Tim 3:1; John 5:3; 1
Pet 1:5, 1:20; Rev 15:1) are at the core of Christian eschatology. The
purpose of this eschatology, that is grounded in revelation theology, and interpreted Christologically and pneumatologically, is
to bring into focus all the consequences of the self-revelation of
the threefold God already contained in the life and works, the
death and resurrection of Jesus of Nazareth. Because the Creator
reveals himself as the consummator of man and the world in
God's eschatological self-mediation in Jesus Christ. That is why
it can be said:

> Eschatology is concrete creation theology. It moves within
> the horizon of God's self-mediation consummated in the
> Christ event. It designates—from the perspective of the

once for all (Heb 7:27)—God's unrepentant self-consent in his Son in these last days (cf. Heb 1:1–3), in whose obedient self-oblation on the cross for us and the pronouncement of his Holy Spirit.

## 2. Questions Treated in Eschatology

The drama of the encounter of God and man in Jesus Christ gives rise to three intersecting sets of questions:

1.  The *individual* eschatology, i.e., the impact on individuals of God's self-mediation from the perspective of free volition and autonomy. This aspect itself relates to the totality of man's earthly existence, but also to death, the particular judgment as well as (possibly) the loving purification and consummation ("purgatorial fire") and, finally, the final destiny of man, either in loving unity with God (= heaven) or in definitive contradiction to God's love (= hell). Pertinent in this context is also the question concerning the "intermediate state" between the death of men as individuals and the general resurrection in the last time.

2.  The *relationship between the Church and eschatology*, i.e., the question regarding to what degree God's eschatological self-mediation impacts the Church as a whole—being, as it is, in Christ, like a sacrament and instrument both of a very closely knit union with God and of the unity of the whole human race (LG 1).

    The eschatological perspective considers the Church as a community of faith, hope and love, as well as prayer for each other, as the communion of saints which encompasses the worldly and already consummate Church. The questions treated here involve, not least, Christian ways of living, either in the decision for marriage as the sacrament of God's steadfast and definitive covenant loyalty or the abstention from marriage and wholehearted service towards the establishment in the Kingdom of God in the final days.

3. *Universal* eschatology: The question of the concernment of man, as an essence endowed with a universal-historical orientation and a creationally innate spiritual-corporeal existence, in the horizon of the second coming of Christ, the universal last judgment, the general resurrection of the dead, the end of history and, finally, the belief in the transcendent act of the recreation or re-establishment of heaven and earth, so that, in the end, Christ is all and in all (Col 3:11) and God rules over all and in all (1 Cor 15:28).

## 3. The Hermeneutics of Eschatological Statements

The eschatology supplies no advance information or even a graphic depiction of events beyond the realm of space and time. Instead, it reflects God's personal self-mediation that calls on man to be resolved in time and history against the horizon of the promised transcendent consummation. That is why eschatological statements require an especially well thought-through hermeneutics. A hermeneutical criterion for eschatological statements is provided by Karl Rahner:

> ... man, as a Christian, knows about his future due to, by means of and in light of the fact that, through God's revelation, he knows himself and his redemption in Christ. His knowledge of the *eschata* is not an appendix to dogmatic anthropology and Christology, but rather nothing other than exactly their transposition into the mode of consummation. Such a prospective draft of one's own Christian existence towards one's future consummation is nevertheless strict revelation, because this revelatory interpretation of human existence is revelation that oc-

curs in God's Word. But it is precisely *in* what man hears about himself from God as the opening of the truth of his existence that the revelation of the future occurs and vice versa. (*Theologische Prinzipien zur Hermeneutik eschatologischer Aussagen*, Schriften IV, 415 f.)

In the words of Hans Urs von Balthasar, this theocentrical, Christocentrical and anthropological enunciation of more recent eschatology can also be summarized as follows:

God is the "last thing" of the creature. Gained, he is heaven; lost, he is hell; examining, he is judgment, purifying, he is purgatory. To him finite being dies, and through and to and in him it rises. But this is God as he presents himself to the world, that is, in his Son, Jesus Christ, who is the revelation of God and therefore the whole essence of the last things. In this way eschatology is, almost more even than any other *locus theologicus*, entirely a doctrine of salvation. (Explorations in Theology I: The Word Made Flesh, San Francisco: Ignatius Press, 1989, 260 f.; Verbum Caro, Skizzen zur Theologie I, 282)

## 4. Important Statements on Eschatology in Church Dogma

The following doctrinal decisions must be interpreted historically and soberly in the overall coherence of the Christian faith (in the hierarchy of truths), in their individual historical context and in terms of the corresponding statement intention (hermeneutics of dogma).

### a) Regarding the fate of individuals

(1.) Death is the result of sin (Decree on Original Sin, Council of Trent, 1546; DH 1512 with a reference to Rom 5:12; GS 18).

(2.) Death is the end of the pilgrim status. After death man can no longer influence his final fate by meritorious deeds (cf. The Errors of Martin Luther treated in the Bull *Exsurge Domine* 1520, Propositio 38, DH 1488).

(3.) To the extent that death expresses distance from grace, the death of Christ is the final triumph over the reign of death (all confessions of faith).

(4.) Immediately following death, particular judgment ensues, deciding the final destiny of beatitude (in heaven) or purification in purgatorial fire or the condemnation to hell (before the corporeal resurrection and Parousia); hence, the final status does not begin on the last day after an intermediate stay in Sheol (cf. Constitution *Benedictus Deus* by Pope Benedict XII, 1336; DH 1000–1002; Union Bull *Laetentur caeli* of the Council of Florence, 1439; DH 1304–1306).

(5.) Doctrine states that heavenly beatitude consists of the enjoyment, the vision and the love of the divine essence (*fruitio, visio et dilectio essentiae divinae*).

Other names for beatitude are heaven, paradise of heaven, native land (DH 839, 1000). God is known in his unity, his triunity and in the processions of the three divine persons, clearly by name, openly and immediately without creaturely mediation; however, this does not mean that we can achieve access to a vision of God in some way other than exclusively *modo creaturae*, through the mediating human nature assumed by the Logos. Even those souls released from the body (i.e., men who are no longer in relation with the old form of the earth and are no longer in the statu viae) see God, as he is, and to the extent they are capable as determined by their status, that after all still awaits the outstanding consummation in the Communion of All Saints in the new earth at the end. At the time of the corporeal resurrection, the body will also participate in the vision of God (cf. Constitution *Benedictus Deus*).

The vision of God is supernatural. Only through the *lumen gloriae*, imparted out of grace, which replaces the *lumen fidei*, are spirit and will able to be raised to the vision of God's essentiality (cf. Council of Vienne, Constitution *Ad nostrum qui*, 1312; DH 895).

For men this vision of God varies in degrees corresponding to their merits. The saint rejoices in it with assurance, and it is eternal and impossible to lose (Constitution *Benedictus Deus*).

It may only be attained immediately after death by those who die in the state of grace of justification and in the love of God and is wholly free of guilt and punishment for sin (Decree on Justification, Council of Trent, 1547; DH 1546; 1582; cf. Vienne; DH 894).

(6.) The doctrine regarding purgatorial fire is that it exists and is the place (status) of the cleansing (purgatorium) of man from any remaining punishments for sin.

It pertains only to Christians who die in the state of justification but who are burdened with residual sin that prevents them from entering a complete union with God in love (Lyon I, 1254; DH 838; Lyon II, 1274; Profession of Faith of the Emperor Michael Palaiologos DH 856-85; Constitution *Benedictus Deus*; Council of Florence 1439, *Laetentur caeli*, DH 1304–1306; Council of Trent, *Decretum de purgatorio* 1563, DH 1820). The souls in purgatorial fire are secure in their salvation (against Luther; *Errores Martini Lutheri*, Prop. 38, DH 1488). In connection with *purgatorium* the image used in the Bible for judgment is fire (*ignis transitorius* or *temporaneus*; DH 838).

(7.) The punishment for the original sin is the loss of the vision of God. Whoever dies without having received the full state of grace of justification received through baptism, suffers only the *poena damni* which is identical with the involuntary abstention from the vision of God and, in the case of the guiltless unchristened, is in accord with a condition of natural beatitude, not the *poena sensus*, i.e., a punishment experienced sensually after the resurrection of the body (cf. the discussion regarding the problem of unbaptized, dying children and the theory of *limbus infantium*; Letter of Pope Innocent III to Humbert of Arles, 1201; DH 780; Florence; DH 1306).

In juxtaposition to these less binding statements, consideration must be given to the more recent conception of the Second Vatican Council regarding the prospect of salvation for those not baptized. This supersedes all limbo theories.

(8.) Regarding hell (*infernum*), doctrine says that it is entered by those who stubbornly persist in a current deadly sin unto death (*Benedictus Deus*, DH 1002; Florence, DH 1306).

What is important is the doctrine of eternity in the punishment of hell. In 543, the Synod of Constantinople accepted the anathemas spoken by the Emperor Justinian against Origen, who in the context of his apocatastasis doctrine referred to a subsequent repentance of the demons and the damned (DH 409; 411).

The reason for eternal damnation is their own, free will (*Fides Pelagii papae*, 557; DH 443), which through *facta capitalia* (Synod of Arles, 473; DH 342) brings down God's rejection because they remain adamantly in the state of the present deadly sin, expressing neither remorse nor penitence, until death (Valence, 855, DH 627; Lyon I, 1245, DH 838; Constitution *Benedictus Deus*, DH 1002; Florence, 1439, DH 1306)

## b) On the communion of the living and the dead in Christ

(1.) All those who belong to Christ are united in a true salvation, whether the saints in heaven, the faithful on their pilgrimage or those souls committed to purification in the purgatorial fire (Pope Leo XIII, Encyclical *Mirae caritatis*, 1902, DH 3360-64; cf. especially also chap. 7 and 8 of the Church Constitution *Lumen gentium*, 1964, and the Annex *communio sanctorum* in the Symbolum Apostolicum as well as the *Explanatio Symboli* of Nicetas of Remesiana, ca. 400, DH 19).

(2.) The consummated saints in heaven pray for men (Trent, DH 1821; 1867). The *cultus duliae* rendered to them (not the *cultus latriae*, i.e., adoration rendered to God alone) is towards the honor of the threefold God who sees himself honored in the men and women blessed by him (Nicaea II, DH 601; Trent, DH 1821–25).

(3.) The souls in the condition of purification participate in the communion of saints. However, they themselves can do nothing for their advancement. But the living can help them in the form of intercession: by celebrating the sacrifice of the mass, by prayer, deeds of active charity and other works of piety (Trent, Decree on the Sacrifice of the Mass, DH 1753; Decree on Purgatorial Fire, DH 1820). Indulgences can also be devoted to them "per modum suffragii" (Sixtus IV, Bull *Salvator noster*, 1476, DH 1398; to their elucidation Sixtus IV, Encyclical *Romani Pontificis provida*, 1477, DH 1405–07; Leo X, Decree *Cum postquam*, 1518, DH 1447–1449). The letter of the Congregation for the Doctrine of the Faith to all bishops regarding the eschatology *Recentiores episcoporum synodi* dated 17 May 1979 emphasizes in this connection that the Church's prayers, "her funeral rites and the religious acts offered for the dead," represent *loci theologici* and that those theological theories that make them appear to be senseless must be rejected (DH 4654).

### c) On universal eschatology

(1.) At the end, Christ returns in his Parousia in the human nature assumed by him as his own (all Symbola). The theory of Chiliasm or Millenialism, a theory according to which Christ in worldly time before the last judgment will establish a visible kingdom for the period of 1000 years (Decree of the Holy Office, 1944, DH 3839) is rejected.

(2.) All men, even the damned, have a share in the resurrection of the dead, to eternal life or the eternal damnation of men in their souls and bodies (*Fides Pelagii papae*, 557, DH 443; Toledo VI, 638, DH 493; Toledo XI, 675, DH 540; Lateran IV, 1215; DH 801; Lyon II, 1274; DH 859; Constitution *Benedictus Deus*, 1336, DH 1002).

All are resurrected in their own flesh (*in propria carne, cum suis propriis corporibus*, DH 801), not in an ethereal or phantom body.

Christ himself and alone awakes the dead (all Symbola), and the grace of Christ, the head of his body, the Church, enters into all members (Pope Vigilius, Letter *Dum in sanctae*, 552, DH 414).

(3.) The resurrection of the dead is followed by the universal judgment over the whole of humanity and its history (all Symbola and documents to date).

This day is unknown to all angels and men. Christ knows this day *in* his human nature, not *from* it but rather only from his divine nature (Pope Gregory I, Letter *Sicut aqua*, 600, DH 474).

This is followed by the material consummation of the world. A theory about *how* this consummation takes place is strictly rejected (Pope Pius II, The Errors of Zaninus de Solcia, 1459, Propositio 1, DH 1361).

At the end is the Kingdom of God and Christ. The blessed live eternally in eternal life. Eternal life is the fruit of the justification, the grace and the merits from good works (Trent, Decree on Justification, DH 1545–47).

The Church passes over into the "heavenly" Kingdom. As a *means* of salvation it will come to an end, but as a *fruit* of salvation, it shall remain (6th Synod of Toledo, 638, DH 493). All Saints reign with Christ for eternity (= united with God's will, i.e., in conformance with love; 11th Synod of Toledo, 675; DH 540; 16th Synod of Toledo, 693, DH 575; Trent, DH 1821; II. Vaticanum, LG 7 and 8); "...his kingdom will have no end" (*cuius regni non erit finis:* cf. Dan 7:14; Luke 1:33; all Symbola, especially the Nicene–Constantinopolitan Creed, 381, DH 150).

## 5. Differences from the Orthodox and Reformed Profession of Faith

Differences in the eschatology only relate to "purgatorial fire." The Orthodox churches did not go through the development of individual eschatology as did the Western Church.

The vision of God or its loss occurs only at the time of the consummation of the world on Judgment Day. According to Orthodoxy, souls remain in *Sheol* in their intermediate state. However, this comprises altogether distinctive degrees rising to the paradise of martyrs and saints.

But the Orthodox churches profess, as does the Catholic Church, that one can pray for the deceased to ease their circumstances. For all who have died having committed venial sins and are then "punished" for them require our help through which they experience relief or, in the end, are even raised into the higher, more blessed regions of Sheol. This controversial question was primarily the subject of negotiations at the Ecumenical Councils of Lyon II (1274) and Florence (1439).

Today, this need no longer be perceived as a doctrinal contradiction necessitating ecclesiastical separation, for the basic ideas of the communion of saints and prayer of intercession are shared by both. On the other hand, it need not be related to a completely congruent model of the relationship between individual and universal eschatology.

The denial of purgatorial fire in the works of Luther and Calvin is based on a wholly different reason. It is the doctrine of justification which, according to the Reformers, is contradicted by the doctrine of indulgence and prayer that is understood to be beneficial for the deceased. The basic principle that the sacrifice of Christ is in every way enough for the forgiveness of sins also appears to contradict the Sacrifice of the Mass for the living and the dead.

As interpreted by Luther and Calvin, Catholic dogma says that mass, prayer and indulgences are man's way of exercising influence on God in order to achieve reconciliation with him. However, reconciliation is a gift from God that we accept and exclusively receive in faith but that we cannot influence by our human efforts.

However, if faith is only understood as the individual's trusting affiliation with Christ and not also as the origin of a new existence whose one fundamental resolve impacts all the multifaceted (including socially relevant) expressions of life, where it proves itself and grows to its full stature, then both good works, taken for themselves, as well as intercession for others are relatively nonfunctional. In this context, clarification can only be provided by a deeper vision of the Church as a salvific congregation, united in Christ, that takes entirely seriously both the individual as well as the social structure of man and his historical nature. Seen in this manner, there has always been a social aspect integral to salvation and redemption in Christ. Against this horizon of understanding, however, prayer for others is itself an avowal of solidarity within the process of salvation, and, as such, a formative consequence of this social dimension.

However, at the time of the Reformation, the former understanding of church as a *communio sanctorum* was considerably faded on the Catholic side. In 1563, in response to Reformation objections, the 25th Session of the Council of Trent succinctly defended traditional Catholic belief in its Decrees on Purgatory and the veneration of the saints, but also rejected all populist and extensively speculative ideas as well.

There is an entirely satisfying answer of the magisterium to the objections from Reformers in *Lumen gentium* Chapter 7: "The eschatological nature of the pilgrim Church and its union with the Church in heaven."

## 6. Christian Eschatology in Association and Contradiction

Eschatology presents the Christian understanding of reality as a whole. That is why in the individual statements regarding the destiny of men and the world always also address all the fundamental questions: the understanding of God, the term revelation, the understanding of the world as creation, especially the image of man, who as a creature is summoned to the supernatural consummation in the grace of God and the supernatural communion with the life of the divine, and who, even in his natural existence (soul and body) is included into the transcendent consummation event.

Despite fundamental differences in their understanding of God, men and the world, outside of Christianity there are—based on general anthropology—outlines of hope of a transcendent consummation, such as the idea of the immortality of the soul or of a mystical dissolution of individual existence in Nirwana, or the hope for an immanent consummation in participating in the advance of humanity as a genus or even that one's own matter belongs to the cosmic life cycle of nature.

## a) Immortality in Greek Philosophy

Greek mythology (Homer, Hesiod) is familiar with the idea of a shadowy existence of the dead in Hades or the withdrawal of individuals chosen by the gods to the blessed site of Elysium.

Following the beginnings in the Orphic-Pythagorean doctrine, the dualistic anthropology, according to which man is composed of two completely different natures, the soul and the body, also was accepted into the major works of Attic philosophy. The concurrent transience and mortality relates to the body, that is woven into matter, while, on the other hand, the soul is the bearer of hope and immortality. Starting from the idea of participation, Plato understands the soul in terms of its ability to comprehend the ideas of the beauty, truth, righteousness and the goodness. Since these ideas are eternal and independent of the fluctuation of appearances, to the degree that the soul is capable of knowing the eternal one, it is also possible to conclude the soul's eternal content. In the realm of ideas the soul pre-exists even prior to its association with the body in which it then enters as a "dungeon." Plato developed his theory of the immortality of the soul based on its inner divine nature in the major dialogs (*Meno, Phaedo, Phaedrus* and *Politeia*):

> ...to escape [from earth] is to become like God, so far
> as this is possible; and to become like God is to become
> righteous and holy and wise...But...let us give the true
> reason: God is in no wise and in no manner unrighteous,

but utterly and perfectly righteous, and there is nothing
so like him as that one of us who in turn becomes most
nearly perfect in righteousness." (*Theaetetus* 176 bc)

In referring back to myth in this context, Plato is also aware of a
judgment of the dead. It is consummated corresponding to the status of the inner freedom achieved contemplatively from the world
for the ideas, and corresponding to doing good and evil. For less
serious crimes, when otherwise one's moral conduct is good, one
may place one's hope in "purification" in the beyond.

The doctrine of Aristotle differs fundamentally from Plato's. For
Aristotle all knowledge begins with sensual perception. He rejects
the idea of knowledge as the recollection of ideas by a pre-existen-
tial soul. In his work *On the Soul* he understands soul and body as
the substantial unity of a single nature. The soul is the *entelechy*
(goal orientation), which realizes and consummates what the body
is in its vigor. A special existence of the soul without body is unimaginable for him. The soul originates and expires with the body.
Aristotle considers any idea of transmigration of souls to be pure
fantasy. Because the difference between bodies in terms of form
and number is grounded specifically in each of their own individual souls, one soul cannot have multiple bodies.

In the Middle Ages, a serious controversy developed over the correct interpretation of the Aristotelian doctrine of the soul. The Islamic
philosopher and Aristotle commentator Averroes (1126–1198) denied
individual immortality and assumed merely the indestructibility of
a universal mind. Thomas Aquinas already criticized this interpretation of Aristotle. Later, then, the Fifth Lateran Council rejected the
Averroismus of Pietro Pomponazzi (1462–1525) and explained that the
immortality of the soul is a reality knowable by reason. What was at
stake here is not the explicit rejection of the immortality of the soul as
such, but its *individual* immortality (DH 1440 f.).

For Aristotle it is an undeniable fact that man's body is subject
to the law of becoming and decaying. Similarly, the passive intellect (*intellectus possibilis*) is capable of suffering and, hence, transient.

Only the active intellect (*intellectus agens*) is not touched by the world. It is not capable of suffering and is, hence, imperishable. As purely cognitive activity, it is divine and eternal. Aristotle appears to have entertained the notion that the active intellect, despite its unity with matter, is to a certain extent independent of the body, and of divine origin, descending into individual men, as it were, from above. At the time of death it returns to its own sphere. Perhaps this is the reason why in Aristotle there is only one *intellectus agens* in all individual men that alone is immortal. What remains questionable is the continued existence of individual men, because individuality cannot be conceived apart from and without corporeity.

A perusal of non-Christian ideas about man's final destiny reveals to some extent a certain degree of continuity towards Christian eschatology as the same existentially basic questions which have been thematized in the first place by man pertaining to the meaning of life in view of suffering, illness and personal death, as well as the goal of history and the world. However, at the same time, a discontinuity becomes visible because the Christian idea of the consummation of man is founded solely on God's self-mediation and the doctrine of individual resurrection assumes an idea of the individual person found in creation theology that is unknown outside of the Judeo-Christian tradition.

### b) The Destruction of Eschatology in Modern Criticism of Christianity

According to the diagnosis provided by Karl Löwith (1897–1973), the positions opposed to Christianity contained in Feuerbach's critique of religion, in Marxism, materialistic evolutionism and in positivism only represent "a secularization of its eschatological predecessor" (*Weltgeschichte und Heilsgeschehen*, St 1953, 11).

In line with Friedrich Nietzsche (1844–1900) and Franz Overbeck (1837–1905), Löwith argues for a complete emancipation of philosophy from theological tradition. In juxtaposition to the Judeo-Christian historical theology with its idea of a beginning and an absolute end of history and its transposition into God's eternity, he takes up the earlier Greek idea of the eternity of the cosmos and the eternal recurrence.

The destructive criticism of Christian eschatology is set in the context of an anthropocentrically immanent view of the world and the disassociation from a fundamental theocentric orientation. The great ideas God, freedom and immortality are assigned to man's self-understanding in a functional sense as conditions which must be postulated functionally as conditions so that man can realize himself as an ethical being. This new idea of man that sees in culture, science and work the fulfillment of the human condition and whose understanding of the divine willfully identifies God as man's competitor can be found as far back as the Renaissance. Its spread was delayed by the religious disputes in the course of the Reformation. However, after the century of the Church schism, it became the underlying current of the European Enlightenment. Religious and metaphysical claim to truth was encountered by an emerging skepticism and deeply felt agnosticism. Religious conviction became a personal matter. In the areas of public life such as the state, jurisprudence, public morals and the economic system, a natural system of knowledge and pragmatic activity took shape. By comparison, the universal, empirically not verifiable, claim of a supernatural revelation was made to appear like a foreign body. It threatened the autonomy of theoretical and ethical reason. The thought of reward or punishment in the afterlife is rejected as inappropriate to true morality and, at times, the attempt is even made to expose it as the instrument of a ruling ideology (the clergy).

In English deism the attempt is made to strip revealed religion of its heteronomous claim (i.e., recourse to a supernatural authority) and to reconstitute it in the framework of autonomous reason as natural religion (M. Tindal, J. Toland). According to Herbert of Cherbury (1583–1648) all concrete historical religions are based on an arsenal of five main convictions, among them the assumption of the existence of a unsurpassably good being and the compensatory righteousness after death according to the principles of reward and punishment.

The contents of a positive religion that goes back to a supernatural revelation, according to this opinion, consist of nothing but aids towards illustrating the truths already knowable by reason, pedagogical aids with which (deistically understood) God wants to direct man for the development of his reasonable nature. What counts is to enlighten man into becoming a reasonable personality, free of prejudices and ethically purified. From this position, G.E. Lessing derived the notion of a possible progress in the world beyond and the statement of belief in the "eternity of the punishment of hell" is rejected as being irreconcilable with God's goodness and his pedagogical goal.

In the course of the epistemological destruction of metaphysics in British empiricism, David Hume, by annulling the term substance, also undermined the traditional argumentation for the immortality of the soul, that had been supported specifically by the indestructibility of a spiritual and immaterial substance. Hume no longer understands the soul as the metaphysical bearer of the spiritual-corporeal nature of man and as the addressee of God's natural and supernatural consummating acts, but rather merely as a bundle of perceptions. It is destroyed as a matter of course when the corporeal functions fail.

Such an understanding of the soul in which one can hear the atomism of antiquity represented by Democritus and Epicurus, and that reduces the inner reality of man to an unusual composition of matter or a functional system of material parts paves the way for materialism. This not only undermines metaphysics, but any sort of eschatology as well.

While Kant, Hegel and Schleiermacher had continued the attempt to mediate classical Christian eschatological statements with the new worldview emerging from the empirical sciences and philosophical rationalism—they remained indecisive or rejective regarding the question of individual immortality—the nineteenth century witnessed a definitive discharge of Christian eschatology in the criticism of religion.

In his work *Gedanken über Tod und Unsterblichkeit* (1830) Ludwig Feuerbach (1804–1872) denies outright the "personal immortality of man." Only the general essence of man is immortal, because it is divine. However, this immortality is not realized beyond history, but rather in its immanence. The general essence of man proves to be the continuously self-transcending tendency towards an immanent goal. The anticipation of this immanent-eschatological goal is experienced by man where he is most intimately connected with his nature, specifically in his sensual-sexual experience of the unity of spirit and nature, or more intensively in the sexual unity of man and woman. The transcendent experience of the loving unity with God is transformed into the sensual-empirical feeling of unity. It is in this way that the eschatological kingdom of God is transferred into the realized general essence of man and into sexual desire in which the merging of the individual with the general is experienced.

Karl Marx (1818–1886) criticized both the thought of reconciliation of the idealistic Christian philosophy as well as the popular Christian idea of a spatially conceived paradise in a world to come as a strategy of consolation with which those benefiting from unjust socio-economic conditions want to delude the exploited about the true reasons for present suffering and hobble the potential for change. Christian eschatology is only the codification of a dual world. This ideologically grounds the alienation of man instead of overcoming it. The criticism of the religion of the world to come is the prerequisite of an active partisanship for a better world on earth:

> The abolition of religion as the *illusory* happiness of the people is the demand for their *real* happiness. To call on them to give up their illusions about their condition is to call on them to give up a condition that requires illusions. The criticism of religion is, therefore, in embryo, the criticism of that vale of tears of which religion is the halo. (Zur Kritik der Hegelschen Rechtsphilosophie, 1843/44: *Frühschriften*, hg. S. Landshut, St 1964, 208)

Marxist philosophy is not the negation of eschatology, but rather its secularized transposition into the dynamic of history onto an immanently worldly "paradise" of reconciled contradictions that is brought about not by the grace of God but by the creative action of men.

So communism is consummated naturalism and humanism, resolution of contradictions of man and nature, of freedom and necessity, individual and genus. "Communism is the riddle of history solved, and it knows itself to be this solution" (*Nationalökonomie und Philosophie,* 1844: ibid. 235)

In non-Marxist philosophy as well, what occurs is an immanentizing of the hope for an eschatological identity of man

In light of the radically experienced finiteness of man, life is interpreted by Martin Heidegger as the steady movement towards death or the fallenness into the-they. Man is called into the authenticity of his existence.

The only way Karl Jaspers sees out of the inauthenticity of existence is in the experience of transcendence as existential elucidation. Man cannot fundamentally change his situation he can only make it more bearable by interpretation.

Sigmund Freud wants to show man the way to an identity with himself by pointing out the necessity of becoming conscious of non-identity through psychoanalysis and the possibility of resolving the negative experiences at the root of this non-identity.

Perhaps no one else expressed more clearly the de-eschatologization of the attitude towards life and, hence, the end of hopes, than Friedrich Nietzsche in his expression "the death of God" that Martin Heidegger interprets as follows:

> The supersensual ground for the supersensual world, conceived as the effective reality of a real entity, has become unreal. That is the metaphysical meaning of the metaphysically conceived word "God is dead." (*Holzwege,* F 1977, 254)

In light of this history of destruction, Christian eschatology can only be redeveloped starting from a radicalized question of man in search of himself.

An impulse for the origin of a hope for transcendent reality ensues from the experience of the *Dialectic of the Enlightenment*. The immanent worldly goals of reason and progress reverse into herd behavior, susceptivity to totalitarianism and the subjection of the spirit to economic restraints. The unimaginable extent of human excesses found its expression in Auschwitz, which has become a metaphor for the highest degree of human perversion possible (Th.W. Adorno). Ernst Bloch was able to talk about a "principle of hope" (*Prinzip Hoffnung*), which aligns concrete human acts and concepts with a utopia.

The monstrous experiences of human depravity in doing evil and in the suffering of the victims brought about a new understanding of the "Longing for the Totally Other" (Max Horkheimer) and, with it, Judeo-Christian theology as the expression of "...hope, that this injustice that characterizes the world might not be left unanswered, that injustice might not have the last word" (*Die Sehnsucht nach dem ganz Anderen*, HH 1970, 61).

## 7. The Rediscovery of Eschatology as a Fundamental Christian Purpose

The eschatological essence of Christianity was only marginally included in the theology of cultural protestantism and liberalism of the nineteenth century. In the famous words of Ernst Troeltsch this meant: "The bureau of eschatology is usually closed." By contrast, Hans Urs von Balthasar described eschatology as the "storm center of the theology of our times" (*The Word Made Flesh: Explorations in Theology I*, 1989, 255; *Umrisse der Eschatologie*, in: *Verbum Caro*, Ei 1960, 276).

The reversal occurred at the end of the nineteenth century and then largely in response to the catastrophe of the First World War that triggered a crisis not only in the enlightenment's optimistic belief in progress, but in the cultural blissfulness of liberal theology and bourgeois Christianity as well (Albrecht Ritschl, Adolf von Harnack). Influenced by Kant, God's kingdom was at this point still understood as a kingdom of goodness whose realization in the course of moral progress could not be stopped and would establish itself as the community of those who, by following the categorical imperative, live the unity of morality and beatitude.

By contrast, Franz Overbeck, a friend of Friedrich Nietzsche, had already emphasized the "otherness, other-worldliness and anti-cultural position of Jesus," that was, he maintained, deeply influenced by the imminent expectation. This imminent expectation, he said, must be seen as virtually the core of Jesus's message of the kingdom of God. He goes on to say that every later attempt to mediate escapism and worldly design, culture and belief is already a regression from Jesus's radical eschatology. For Overbeck, however, this knowledge was not the occasion for the renewal of theological eschatology. Instead, he thought that Jesus had been deluded, and he drew the consequence for himself and distanced himself from Christian belief as a historical error (*Über die Christlichkeit unserer heutigen Theologie*, 1873, Da 1963).

But, for theology, the book by Johannes Weiß (1863–1914) was virtually epoch-making: *Die Predigt Jesu vom Reiche Gottes* (Gö 1892).

From then on, the reflection on Jesus's proclamation of the Kingdom of God became the focal point, the thesis of the imminent expectation and the delay of the Parousia became theology's main problem.

From these clusters of questions emerged new basic concepts of eschatology:

(1.) *Consistent eschatology.* Its representatives, Johannes Weiß, Albert Schweitzer and Martin Werner, assume that Jesus had placed his hope in an apocalyptic and futuristic imminent expectation, that the kingdom would penetrate into the world from above in the very near future. After the death of Jesus, the congregation kept alive the imminent expectation. The delay of the Parousia, however, led to eschatologizing the proclamation of the kingdom of God and, as a result, to its transformation into a dogmatic and moralistic system influenced by Hellenism.

**(2.)** *Realized eschatology* (C.H. Dodd) sees the kingdom of God fulfilled in Christ's cross and resurrection. Any statements about dates are secondary. The futuristic dimension is merely the opening of a way to the eschatological unity with God which has already begun now.

**(3.)** The transcendental-actualistic eschatology of *Karl Barth* (in the early days of dialectical theology) has the trumpets of the last judgment sound over liberal cultural Christianity and the theology of history: "Christianity that is not irreducibly eschatological has entirely and altogether nothing to do with Christ" (Karl Barth, *The Epistle to the Romans*, trans. E.C. Hoskyns, Oxford 1933, p. 314; *Der Römerbrief,* M 21922, 298).

The eschatological hope of Christianity does not refer teleologically to the end of time and history at the time of the Parousia, but rather it is the expression of the radical dialectic of time and eternity. It designates the forever and the now of the divine claim and becomes the crisis of man and his historically continuous self-realization in time. Man is not moving in a historically linear direction between the "already" and the "not yet." On the contrary, God's eternity penetrates repeatedly each moment of time and radically challenges man. God's word is simultaneously man's limit, crisis and orientation in radical contradiction to man's religious path from himself to God.

**(4.)** *Rudolf Bultmann* understands the temporally imminent expectation and the concrete cosmic and eschatological statements of the end of the world as elements of a superseded mythical worldview. It is not possible to simply ignore them. But their actual content should be unlocked by means of an *existential interpretation.* The message of Jesus calls me to decide and, hence, to enter the authenticity of my existence. The encounter with Jesus situates me in the here and now in relation to the end of the world and, at the same time, brings me into the newly created existence of decisiveness. In this way the basis of my ability to exist blossoms into freedom. It is necessary to abstain from objectively historical salvific facts and professions of faith or even to suggest that they can be verified by empirical science. Hence, faith is also independent of objections or confirmations of a worldview and natural science. Jesus Christ is the eschatological event (*Die christliche Hoffnung und das Problem der Entmythologisierung*, St 1954, 58; Rudolf Bultmann, *The Christian Hope and the Problem of Demythologizing:* ExpTim 65 (1953–54), 228–30, 276–78).

(5.) In his understanding of salvation as history *Oscar Cullmann* turns to the historical, secular and social points of the Gospel that are implied in the eschatological proclamation of the kingdom of God. Lukas portrays Jesus Christ as the "middle of time." From the present he encompasses the dimensions of past and future. Present and future eschatology no longer diverge as mutually opposing moments. The resurrection of Jesus is a guaranty of our future resurrection that remains the outstanding object of our hope. In a linear understanding of time, individual events are identified as God's revelatory acts. Christ stands between the "already fulfilled" and the "yet to be fulfilled." Thus, the *eschata* are also related to the external events at the beginning and end of time and history.

(6.) In his universal history approach, *Wolfhart Pannenberg* sees man's self-understanding as being grounded in a mediation between the reference to God and relationship with the world. Belief is related to real history and not to the mere *that* of an empty historicity as in abstract existentialism. In the words of Scripture the interpretation of the events occurs as God's self-revelation. Their consummation will not be achieved until the unveiling of the final event at the end of history. For Pannenberg, then, universal history is the framework in which we could comprehend individual historical events, including the history of Jesus, especially the historical events of his resurrection from the dead, as partial moments. However, Pannenberg understands Christ's resurrection as prolepsis and anticipation of the end of history. So believers are really mediated by the universal-historical horizon in which the acceptance of the mortal man in Christ by the trinitarian God becomes evident. This perspective of hope, he writes, is the answer to the question that man is to himself.

(7.) The *theology of liberation*, which itself has received important impulses from a theology of hope (Jürgen Moltmann) as well as from political theology (Johann Baptist Metz), attempts to recapture the eschatological dimension of Christian belief by protesting its marginalization into the private sphere and its reduction to interiority, against an ethics of conviction and its misuse as an ideology of consolation. In practice, Jesus's kingdom of God encompasses especially the secular realities such as the liberation of the poor and enslaved as well the judgment on the exploiters. Nevertheless, apart from a few popularizations without any theological authority, Jesus is not understood primarily as a social revolutionary. The eschatological hope, to the contrary, becomes the driving force of world-changing praxis in the participation in the praxis of Jesus. The memory of past suffering also becomes the potential for change. At the same time, it draws past generations into the universal hope placed in the God of salvation who, on the cross of Jesus, took the suffering of the world upon himself and, in the resurrection of Jesus from the dead, revealed his grace as a world-changing power. Hence, ecclesiastic activity is not reconverted by the theology of liberation for the creation of an inner-worldly paradise. On the contrary, it is the participation in the eschatological, the world in history and the transforming and liberating acts of God into eternity.

# 8. Categories of Thinking in Current Eschatology

## a) Theocentricity, Christocentricity, Anthropocentricity

Creation theology is the context from which the idea arises that, in the order of its material and spiritual principles, the world is focused on man. Man, who subsists in spiritual-corporeal nature is also the bearer of the self-transcendence of the whole creation both in his origin as well as in his goal.

In man the *anthropocentricity* of the world goes beyond itself to become a *theocentricity* of man, to the extent that man is constituted in the first place by his self-transcendence towards God.

In an unsurpassable manner the encounter of man and God takes place in Jesus Christ. The self-expression of God incarnated in his Son, on the one hand, and the self-commendation of the man Jesus—representing all of mankind to God, on the other, constitute the linchpin of salvation history and mediate the anthropocentricity of creation with the theocentricity of man.

This is how *Christocentricity* becomes a decisive dimension both of ecclesiastic practice and theological reflection.

## b) Encounters in Dialog with God

Dialogue is innate to the creature man. Only in language, in the word, does he come into his own. But he does not come to himself in the self-expression in order to relate to other persons as well in the medium of language. Man experiences himself as the being that first becomes aware of itself through the act of being addressed by another. That is why Romano Guardini, merly by considering the order of creation, was able to say:

> The impersonal, the lifeless and alive alike, is created by God simply as immediate object of his will. The person he cannot create like this, nor does he want to, because it would be senseless. He creates the person by an act that anticipates and is the basis of his dignity, that is, by a call. (*Welt und Person*, Wü 21940, 114)

In the incarnation of the Logos God makes himself the bearer of a history of divine-human communication. This responsorial event finds its continuation in the proclamation statement of the Church, that is answered by the profession of faith of the congregation, and in the sacraments as real-symbolic realizations of the divine-human dialog. Man, newly created in Christ, participates in his filial relationship with the Father in the presence and grace of the Spirit in which the communion of Father and Son occurs as love (cf. Rom 8:15, 8:29; Gal 4:4–6; 1 John 1–3 and passim).

### c) Corporeal-wordly constitution of the message of salvation

Under the conditions of the creation and even the incarnation of God, it is not a redemption *from* the world that can be expected of Christianity, but rather a redemption of the world and man. When man dies, his corporeal constitution and personal intercommunication are not shed, but rather consummated in communion with God and other men. That is why the Christian hopes for his "corporeal resurrection" as well as "a new heaven and a new earth."

### d) The future as a dimension of the salvific present

Eschatological salvation is present in the midst of the realization of man's personhood through the event of redemption and its mediation in faith, baptism and church membership. But man, a material, social and historical being, must also always integrate the future into his actualization of existence: He understands the historical future as the horizon against which he recovers himself in the multidimensionality of his creaturely reality and in which God has bestowed himself upon him as the absolute transcendent future. The shaping of his own life as well as social action in responsibility for the world is accomplished towards a still open historical and transcendent future. God's eschatological salvific presence in Jesus Christ—in the world and in man's heart—does not devalue man's concrete historical action, nor does it threaten or hamper it. Instead, it is the reason for hope, courage and confidence. It does not instill in Christians fear of the near end of history but rather hope and prayer for it: "Marána tha—Our Lord, come!" (1 Cor

16:22; Rev 22:20). Eschatology does not contain the warning of an incipient world catastrophe ("twilight of the Gods") nor does it favor a mood of world apocalypse ("the last days of humanity").

Eschatology is the gospel of God's self-revelation as the consummator of his creation.

# II

# THE ESCHATOLOGY OF
# GOD'S SELF-REVELATION
# IN BIBLICAL TESTIMONY

## 1. Adventist Eschatology in the Old Testament

The individual aspects of eschatology begin appearing gradually over the course of the revelation of the Old Testament. Nevertheless, taken as a whole, they do not form a loose conglomerate of heterogeneous images and ideas. They have their center of gravity in God's self-revelation as the salvation of his people in the midst of history.

This development was determined by the increasingly clear knowledge of the consequences that ensue from the revealed understanding of God as well as the reflection on certain basic historical experiences. This is how, gradually, the formation of both the individual eschatology with the hope for the resurrection of the dead, an ecclesiastic eschatology, that taught seeing the people of the covenant as the indestructible sign and tool of God's salvific will, and finally the universal eschatology with its hope for a recreation of heaven and earth, came to pass.

### a) Yahweh, the God of Salvation

Yahweh is experienced as the origin and guarantor of salvation that is knowable in the gifts of long life, community in the family and the clan. In the beginning, there is still hardly any thought given to a hereafter, a salvation after death. Abraham experiences God's blessing in the promise of land and in his vocation to become the patriarch of many peoples (Gen 12). The rescue of Israel from Egyptian slavery is confirmed in the underlying experience of the Yahweh's historically powerful salvific presence. He guarantees the future as a space of the promise of salvation. His "name forever" is: "I am there for you" (Exod 3:14) in graciousness, mercy and fidelity (Exod 34:6). He himself lives as the fulfillment and promise in the midst of his people (Num 35:34). Even despite Israel's failure and injustice towards its covenant, God offers himself in the messianic promise of salvation as the redemption of his historically effective salvific will (2 Sam 7:12–16).

## b) Transposition of the Yahweh hope in prophetic theology

Before the major watersheds in the Israelite history, the destruction of the northern kingdom (722 BC) and the Babylonian exile of Juda (587 BC), the eschatological thought cannot be found that the future could include a definitive end of history. It is the unlimited horizon into which events are continuously unfolding. Against this horizon God acts as the Lord of History, who in the events holds at the ready salvation and blessing, rescue and triumph or judgment and punishment.

In the course of major catastrophes, the image of the relationship of the people to God changes. Calamity is now understood as the expression of judgment and punishment for Israel's turning away from the God of salvation and blessing.

Two decades before the collapse of the northern empire, Amos was already talking for the first time about the "the day of Yahweh," warning of the awful judgment on the hollowing out of cultic rituals and the veneration of foreign gods, the fast and easy lifestyle and decadence of the rich as well as the exploitation of the poor and, finally, the illusory trust in alliances with pagan peoples. The day of judgment would reveal God's no to an Israel that persists in its no to Yahweh, its God. The threat is, however, not an indication of an ambiguity in God's essence but is intended to bring about the repentence of the people. The faithful remnant of Israel (Amos 9:12; Isa 4:3) that has passed through judgment becomes the bearer of the salvific promise at the end of days. Judgment is God's way of bringing about his salvation and breaking open the way to a new period of salvation that will never again end (cf. Jer 3:21 f., 4:1 f., 31:2–5, 31:18–22; Ezek 40:48; Isa 40:1–9 and 54:7–10). This radically new horizon of the Yahweh hope can only be expressed in the category of recreation. Just as the creation was an absolute beginning (Gen 1:1), so will God's definitive salvific action in the midst of history be the constitution of "new heavens and a new earth" (Isa 65:17; Ezek 36). It will be the time of the new and eternal covenant (Jer 31:31–34; Hos 11:8; Ezek 37:26) in which the units of Yahweh and the people of the covenant will be so intimately close that they can be described in the imagery of the love of wife and husband (Hos 2:18–25; Isa 62:4). In this new covenant Jerusalem (Isa 52:1) will become the center of the nations who will pilgrim to Zion (Isa 2:2–4; Mic 4:1–5) to experience there the peace and salvation of Yahweh (Isa 60:2; Zech 2:14 f.). It will be the time of the new paradise (Isa 11:6–9). God himself will come as King and wield the scepter in his kingdom of righteousness (Jer 23:5 f.; Isa 32:1).

This eschatological reign of God will be installed by "David's Son," the anointed (Messiah), who shall proceed as ruler from the city of kings, Bethlehem (Mic 5:1–5), to rule as the shepherd and lord of his people (Ezek 34:23 f., 37:24 f.). He will proclaim the redemption and liberation that Yahweh himself accomplishes (Isa 61:1–3). The question remains open whether the messianic reign of God means the permanent and final inner-worldly end of history, or if this also refers to a view of a transcendent consummation of the creation.

## c) The dramatization of the Yahweh-hope in the apocalypse narrative

Between the political insignificance of Israel and the factual threat it faces, on the one hand, and the prophetic promises, on the other, a discrepancy becomes visible which can hardly be bridged.

The promised reign of God was opposed by the power of hostile groupings. The struggle between God's salvific will and the anti-divine powers could only be comprehended in the categories of universal history or even cosmology. The historical drama taking shape was interpreted as the wrestling of the opposites of belief and non-belief, love and hate, or as the struggle with invisible anti-messianic powers such as the devil and, later, the "Antichrist," etc., who influence the decisions of men. The texts, writings and instances of reformulation that resulted from reflection on these tensions, and that are marked by the "eschatologizing" of theological themes as well as, in regards to their manner of presentation, draw from a vast wealth of images, are usually summarized under the general term of "apocalyptic literature."

In those parts of the OT marked by apocalyptic thinking (Ezek 38; Joel 4:9–17; Zech 13; Dan 2; Isa 24–27), but also in the non-canonical books (cf. the Ethiopian Enoch, the Book of Jubilees, the Ezra Books, the Testaments of the 12 Patriarchs, the Assumption of Moses and the Syriac Apocalypse of Baruch) the hope in Yahweh assumes universal historical, eschatological and cosmic traits. By means of the apocalypse eschatology changes course in the direction of an end of history and its supersession in a transcendental goal. The future is no longer hidden to the believer because he knows of the divine salvific plan that guides the course of history without fail to its final goal. In the canonic and non-canonic apocalyptic narrative, which also includes the writings of the Qumran Community, there are images, series of motives and forms of expression, that are also intended to illustrate the New Testament eschatology. For, impressed by the Jewish war (AD 66–70; cf. Mark 13), and, later, mainly by the exposure to the persecution of the early Christian communities in Asia Minor (cf. Rev) apocalyptic images and motives were also drawn more intensively to depict a christologically conceived eschatology. In detail it is necessary to remember

a. the image of the *final struggle* between God and the forces arraigned against God (Satan, demons, the anti-Messiah or the idea of the contradiction between the old and the new eon, at the end of which a cosmic catastrophe stands with the destruction of evil;

b. the *impatient expectation* of God's near triumph (imminent expectation); the hope of an acceleration of the course of history by God, who should bring about the last judgment soon; this is also related to the problem of the delay of the Parousia in the NT;

c. the expectation of the *last judgment* over the peoples and individuals with reward and punishment for good or evil deeds as well as the establishment of the new paradise;

d. the image of the *transition period* at the end of the old and the advent of a new age. In this intermediate period Yahweh will not yet rule directly and immediately but be represented by the Messiah (Son of Man);

e. the hope that God's reign (the *basileia*) will be brought about that will be accompanied by all imaginable salvific goods such as national freedom and unity and an existence free of suffering and misery.

## d) Hope of postmortal existence

### Yahweh and the dead

The fate of the individual person is certainly given attention in the Old Testament. However, one must not approach the texts with the expectations influenced by modern individualistic anthropocentricity. The individual knows himself first as a member of God's chosen people. And he, like every other living creature, is mortal. Death carries him to *Sheol*, the land of no return (Job 7:9, 38:17), into the shadowy existence of the realm of the dead (Isa 14:10). Although Yahweh's power does not come to an end at the border of Sheol (Ps 139:8), he no longer has an effect on man (Ps 88:6). In Sheol God's praise falls silent (Ps 6:6, 88:11 f.). It is the place without a connection to God (later on, Qoh 3:20). God rules over the living, and he is their God. Nevertheless, a person who prays can beg Yahweh for rescue in the face of death and express the hope that the lasting separation from him in Sheol is not the last word. Occasionally, the hope is expressed (Ps 49 and 73), to be saved from Sheol and be accepted into the God's glorious splendor as Enoch, whose gathering up by God is told in Gen 5:21-24 and how the prophet Elijah, who "went up to heaven" (2 Kgs 2:11 f.).

### The corporeal resurrection

The post-exilic, slowly germinating hope of a postmortal existence is rooted in the belief in Yahweh itself and is not a heterogeneous supplement to it. However, not until the apocalyptic writings (around 250 BC) is the thought of corporeal resurrection expressed explicitly. This does not mean that the idea of the immortality of the soul is complemented by the additional saving of the body as well. Instead, a holistic anthropology, on the one hand, and the belief in God's power to create and save, on the other, are the statement's horizons of understanding. If Yahweh saves man after his death, he saves him in his existence as a living essence consisting of dust and the divine breath of life (Gen 2:7).

The Isaiah-Apocalypse 25:8 knows that Yahweh will destroy death forever, that "the dead shall live" and "their corpses shall rise" (Isa 26:19). The only clear testimony of the belief in resurrection is in Dan 12:1–3:

> ...It shall be a time unsurpassed in distress since the nation began until that time. At that time your people shall escape, everyone who is found written in the book. Many of those who sleep in the dust of the earth shall awake; Some to everlasting life, others to reproach and everlasting disgrace...

Similarly, before his martyr's death by King Antioch, one of the seven Maccabaean brothers is able to say: "It is my choice to die...with the hope that God will restore me to life" (2 Macc 7:14).

Turning to the profession of faith in the God of creation, who with his limitless power made the world from nothing (2 Macc 7:28), Israel comes to the faith-based conviction of the "God's omnipotent judgment" and the "divine assurance of eternal Life" for those who suffer death to sanctify his name.

## Israel's Resurrection

The connection of salvation of the individual with the salvation of the people remains intact as the fundamental idea. In a vision, the prophet Ezekiel sees how the bones of Israel's dead arise from the dead. God makes his people come out of their graves and brings them back to the land of Israel so that they shall know that he is the Lord (Ezek 37:11–14). The interpretation of this text is controversial. The discussion revolves around whether he intends the restoration of Israel after the shame of exile to be understood originally as a metaphor or as an actual corporeal resurrection of the dead.

### The incorruptibility and immortality of man

In the Book of Wisdom (approx. 50 BC), under the influence of Hellenistic anthropology (with the dualistic idea of man as a composite of two different natures of soul and body), the author can speak of the incorruptibility of man, that is, however, grounded in creation theology. "For God formed us to be imperishable; the image of his own nature he made us" (Wis 2:23). Despite the acceptance of the term soul, in this case what is meant is not the immortality of the soul as a substantially divine element, as found for example in Plato. What is involved here is man as the creature of God who can place his hope in immortality (Wis 3:4), because his soul is secure in God's hand. Knowledge of God and the righteousness of the covenant are the "root of immortality" (Wis 15:3) and reason for "incorruptibility" (Wis 6:18).

No uniform idea regarding the resurrection of the dead had developed in Judaism until the time of Jesus. In contrast to the Pharisees, the Sadducees reject it (cf. Matt 22:23; Acts 23:8).

## *The places where the dead are gathered*

The more clearly it is recognized that the life of piety and righteousness led by the deceased is the reason for their beatifying closeness to God, the more crucial became a differentiation in the image of the world of the dead, Sheol (Hades). Thus, the upper area of Hades is described as heaven, paradise, the new Jerusalem or Mount Zion while the place for sinners, the lowest level in the realm of the dead, appears as hell, Gehinnom, valley of the damned, sea of fire, abyss and place of cold and gloom.

But it can also break asunder the linchpin holding together the two parts of a comprehensive idea of Sheol. Heaven, where God reigns over the angels, is then a place already maintained for the blessed, but hell is the place of damnation. These places (*receptacula animarum*) are where the souls of the deceased stay until the general judgment and the general resurrection of the dead.

Finally, this is also coupled with the idea of an intermediate state of the dead after their death. In death they are in personal proximity to or distance from God and, in the last time, expect the complete recreation of the (new) creation as well as the consummation in their corporeal existence.

## *Intermediate state, purification, intercession, prayer*

What also follows from the idea of an intermediate state between the particular and general judgment is the possibility of an intercession for the dead, to ease their condition in the beyond, if it is still afflicted with certain sins and shortcomings. Judas Maccabaeus has purification offerings for the fallen soldiers of Israel with whom idols have been found:

> For if he were not expecting the fallen to rise again, it would have been superfluous and foolish to pray for the dead. But if he did this with a view to the splendid reward that awaits those who had gone to rest in godliness, it was a holy and pious thought. Thus he made atone-

ment for the dead that they might be absolved from their
sin. (2 Macc 12:44–46)

## 2. The Core of the New Testament's Eschatology in the Proclamation of the Kingdom of God by Jesus

### a) The Proclamation of the Reign of God as the New Centering Approach

The divergent eschatological and apocalyptic ideas of the Judaism
of the day are summarized, corrected and centered by Jesus. The
center of Jesus's message is the proclamation of the nearness of
God's kingdom in the fullness of time (Mark 1:15). Jesus's doctrine
and action with God's authority (Mark 2:10) proves him to be the
eschatological mediator of God's salvific reign. He works the signs
for the presence of the eschatological kingdom of God:

> The blind regain their sight, the lame walk, lepers are
> cleansed, the deaf hear, the dead are raised, the poor
> have the good news proclaimed to them. (Luke 7:22; cf.
> Isa 35:5, 42:7, 61:1)

Jesus did not precisely define the meaning of the term "the
kingdom of God." But he distinguishes this from empirically and
historically comprehensible human power structures and empires
and calls it a kingdom that does not belong to this type of world
(John 18:36), that does not come ostentatiously (Luke 17:20). To the
contrary, in the proclamation of Jesus the kingdom of God is the
dynamically unfolding advancement of salvation in the word and
acts of God in the present from which man lets himself be encompassed in the midst of his personal existence in order to experience
God's salvation in the corporeal and social dimension of human existence. Hence, it is possible to refer simultaneously to the presence

of the reign of God (Mark 1:15) and to its coming (Matt 6:9, Luke 11:2) for which Jesus taught his disciples to pray. God's reign is now, in the midst of the world, effective and can be experienced in faith. However, it remains hidden from non-believers and is not revealed in transcendental consummation as the universal reign of God until after death and the general end of history at the last judgment (cf. Matt 25:34, 26:29; 1 Cor 15:28 and passim). Since God's kingdom is not an empirically comprehensible entity, it can also not be evoked primarily in terms of spatial and temporal categories. What is decisive is the dynamic interaction of God's salvific will with man's faith-based obedience. But that is why, in the eschatology, all hypostatized statements about spatial and chronological relations must be interpreted from the perspective of this personal relation between God and man and not vice versa.

Statements about the date of the transcendent complete realization of God's kingdom are not part of Christ's revelatory mission:

> But of that day or hour, no one knows, neither the angels
> in heaven, nor the Son, but only the Father. (Mark 13:32)

But the Kingdom of God definitively comes into the world when Jesus submits completely to the will of his divine Father. This is how obedience to his mission unto the cross becomes the eschatological triumph of the Kingdom of God in the existence of his human mediator (Mark 14:36).

In the sending of the Son the Kingdom of God has definitively entered the world:

> But if it is by the Spirit—the finger—of God that I drive
> out the demons, then the kingdom of God has come
> upon you. (Luke 11:20; cf. Matt 12:28)

Through the obedience of Jesus, the man, who is the representation of the kingdom of God and the voice of man's profession of faith at the head of the new humanity, the basileia has definitively dawned. In this sense he is revealed as the Son of God in the Holy Spirit through the Father's act of resurrection (Rom 1:3; Gal 1,16).

But he is as the representative of humanity simultaneously the eschatological man, the "first of the reawakened" and the "revitalizing Spirit" (1 Cor 15:20, 15:45 ff.). He, as the Son mediator embodying the divine reign of God in the world, due to his proclamation, his death on the cross and resurrection, is the "one mediator between God and man" (1 Tim 2:5). The Son, who learned obedience from what he suffered, achieved consummation and for all those who obey him (who believe in him), "the source of eternal salvation" (Heb 5:9) and became the "high priest" and "mediator of a new covenant" (Heb 8:6; 9:11, 9:15).

In Jesus, God's kingdom takes place in the world because, at the end of days and in the fullness of time, he was sent and revealed himself as the Son of God (Heb 1:1–3). In his destiny as man unto the cross he became "the leader and perfecter of faith" (Heb 12:2), who himself has become the kingdom of God.

In early Christianity, eschatology is understood as an aspect of the Christ event. It includes the transcendent consummation of man's understanding of God as grounded in Christ and, hence, the hope for the Parousia. Then the reign of God and Christ (1 Cor 15:28) is revealed to all men. Until the final, second coming of Christ, the consummation takes effect in faith and love. This leads neither to resignation nor—least of all—to escapism, but rather releases in believers a dynamic of action for the love of one's neighbor and engagement in the world as well as for the universal proclamation of the good news of salvation. The span between the reign of God already initially realized in Christ and its complete revelation at the moment of the Parousia is presented in early Christianity in temporal and spatial thought models. But since the temporal component is not the essence of early Christian eschatology, the Parousia delay (in a temporal sense) was not the occasion of a deep crisis in faith. However, it was in part forgotten how the christological and pneumatological presence of the salvation, on the one hand, and the hope for transcendent consummation in God's absolute future, on the other hand, are related, so that eschatology, although an essential character of the revelation in Christ itself, was for a long time treated separately at the end of the dogmatics in the treatise on the "Doctrine of the Last Things."

## b) Eschatology as understood in the Synoptic Gospels

The Q Sayings contain the penitential sermon of the Baptist at the beginning (Luke 3:7–9). It ends with the word of the last judgment over the twelve tribes (Luke 22:28–30, 17:22–37).

Jesus is identified as the Son of Man (Dan 7:13; Luke 7:34 and passim) and is understood to be eschatological revealer of the Father and the historical agency of the reign of God (Luke 10:21 f.). The behavior towards him in belief or disbelief decides the fate of man and, in particular, of the people of God, Israel (Luke 14:15–24; Matt 22:1–10). He is anticipated as the world judge who at the end of the world will suddenly arrive on the clouds of heaven (i.e., from God).

Through the rejection of the people Jesus must accept the path of the suffering Son of Man (Mark 8:38). Having endured the passion, the awakened Lord proves to be the judge as well. Not until the Parousia will all men comprehend his true significance. Those who follow Christ in his suffering and cross and profess their faith in him as the Son of Man will be saved.

Matthew knows in Jesus the fulfillment of the eschatological promise of the reign of God. The resurrected Lord remains present and effective in his congregation until the consummation of the world (Matt 28:19). All God's sovereignty and power over the world has been conveyed to him. The disciples are the true Israel and the eschatological community of salvation that is called to the universal proclamation of the gospel, the saving service of the forgiveness of sins and succession. At the second coming of the Son of Man for the last judgment the disciples must also be judged by the standard of love, especially the love of one's neighbor (cf. Matt 25).

Luke emphasizes the "today" of salvation. The "epoch of the Church" begins with the death and resurrection of Jesus. In the presence of the Holy Spirit, which the raised Christ sends from the Father into the Church and into the world, the kingdom of God and the gospel of Christ can be spread to the limits of the earth (Acts 28:31). The specification of dates and empirical earthly ideas such as the establishment of a theocracy in Israel are rejected (Acts 1:6 f.). The history of the Church is accomplished within the scope of world history. The role of the Church in the history of humanity is determined by God's resolution to carry out his salvific will in history and the world. Luke is especially interested in the individual salvation of man that can be already fully realized in death and after death (Luke 12:16–21, 16:19–31, 23:43). Nevertheless, the Parousia and the universal consummation still constitute the vanishing point of all individual eschatological statements.

## c) Eschatological Statements in the Pauline Epistles

Paul sees in the cross and in the resurrection of Jesus the turning point of history. Through the sending of the Son of God and his birth as man the *fullness of time* has come (Gal 4:4–6). Jesus is the fulfillment of all of God's promises (2 Cor 1:20; Gal 3:16). Law, sin and death as the powers of the ancient Aion are overcome. As the final form of the new man, as the last Adam, Christ is raised (1 Cor 15:20 ff., 15:45 ff.; Rom 5:12–21) by God who restores life to the dead (Rom 4:17). God placed the curse brought about by sin on Jesus and judged him as a substitute (1 Cor 5:21; Gal 3:13) to reveal man's alienation from God and dissipation. But the revelation of the judgment of sin in the death of Christ—in our stead—is at the same time also the beginning of the new period of salvation in the re-awakening of Christ and all of those who belong to him in faith. Whoever lives in Christ has become a new creature (2 Cor 15:17; Gal 6:15). Justified, reconciled and sanctified, the Christian lives in the Holy Spirit and can overcome the seductive powers of the old existence (the flesh) (Gal 5:16–24; Rom 8:12–14). He lives in the spirit of freedom and in the hope of the final revelation of being a child of God "with the redemption of our body" (Rom 8:18–23).

History comes to the end, when the Son "hands over the kingdom to his God and Father, when he has destroyed every sovereignty and every authority and power," "so that God may be all in all" (1 Cor 15:24–28).

All questions relating to death, judgment and the end of the world are answered by Paul in the light of Christology. The shortness of time and the preliminary nature of this life do not lead to a devaluation of man's worldly existence. They merely intensify the expectation of Christ's Parousia (1 Thess 5:11; Rom 13,11–14). What is decisive is to belong to Christ in life and in death (Rom 14:7). After his death, the believer is with or in Christ (2 Cor 5:1–10; Phil 1:21–23; 1 Thess 4:17).

· By pointing to the Parousia of Christ and the presence of the resurrected Lord, Paulus can console the Church regarding the death of their individual members (1 Thess 4:13–18). Through Jesus, God will also "bring with him those who have fallen asleep to glory" (1 Thess 4:14). At the time of the Parousia "the dead in Christ will rise" (4:16).

In 1 Cor 15, the central resurrection chapter, Paul explains the relationship of the earthly body of the dead to the consummation of man in the corporeal resurrection. "It is sown a natural body; it is raised a spiritual body" (15:44). The corruptible body is, as it were, merely the seed, that through the "life-giving spirit" of Christ will be consummated as the spiritual and glorified, incorruptible and immortal body of the elect in the "kingdom of God" (1 Cor 15:35–53). Due to the justification through the crucifixion and the resurrection of Jesus believers are delivered from the coming wrath (1 Thess 1:10). On the day of God's wrathful judgment "the work of each will come to light... It will be revealed with fire, and the fire [itself] will test the quality of each one's work" (1 Cor 3:13).

When works and deeds are judged, the eternal life will become knowable as reward for the good (Rom 2:7), or God's holiness will be known as wrath (Rom 2:8). At some time "we must all appear before the judgment seat of Christ, so that each one may receive recompense, according to what he did in the body, whether good or evil" (2 Cor 5:10).

## d) Eschatology in the Deutero-Pauline Epistles (universality, the delay of the Parousia)

In the letters to the Colossians and Ephesians graphic spatial and cosmic categories stand out. Salvation, so to speak, awaits in heaven. The Christian moves in his disposition and way of life as if already in heaven (Col 3:3). He has already been buried with Christ and resurrected (Col 2:12). However, from heaven he expects Christ as the savior, so that all appear "in glory" (Col 3:4) and receive their final form.

The Church should make known to all men (Eph 3:10 f.) how the mystery of God's salvation plan (Eph 1:9) was fulfilled in its sum total of creation and history by Christ. The whole fullness of Christ inhabits the Church (Eph 1:23; Col 2:10). He is the head and has made the Church into his body. In him the faithful grow towards him, through him he also wants to give himself to the world, to include all men as members in his body and thus to consummate them (Eph 3:1–13, 4:13).

However, the world is also the field of battle against the forces ranged in opposition to the divine. In the armor of God, the Christian can, clothed in righteousness, faith and the gift of salvation, stand firm in the spiritual struggle against the spirits of evil and the rulers and powers of gloom (Eph 6:10–20).

In reaction to the delay of the Parousia the current affliction is interpreted as a sign of the coming judgment passed on the unbelievers and the objection to the gospel of Christ (2 Thess 1:4–10).

In 2 Thess 2:1–12 the apostle must grapple with the erroneous doctrine, the "day of the Lord" is at hand (2 Thess 2:1–12): Man can only know the signs of the last days, but, first, the widespread abandonment of faith will take place. The lawless one shall come first, who exalts himself above everything that is called God or is sacred and seeks to displace God in the temple (2 Thess 2:4). By means of his lie he will tempt many to abandon Christ; but he shall destroy him when he appears at the time of the Parousia. More important than questions involving the date of the eschatological

events, in this context is the call to vigilance in faith and attentive-
ness to the signs of the time.

In the Pastoral Epistles the delay of the Parousia is not considered a problem. The congregation is waiting for the future consummation at the "Epiphania Christi" (1 Tim 6:16; 2 Tim 4:1, 4:8; Titus
2:13). The judgment is in the future (2 Tim 4:1, 4:8) as is "eternal life"
(1 Tim 1:16; 4:8, 6:12; Tit 1:2, 3:7). The eternal life has been promised by the true God since the beginning of time, and it is now the
foundation of all hope and confidence in faith and in true worship
of God (Titus 1:1 f.).

### e) Other Epistolic Literature

The appearance of the erroneous doctrine is a sign that the end of
days has begun and the Church has entered into an eschatological
probation (Jude 3).

The suffering caused to Christians by hostile surroundings is
experienced by the congregation as a test and a purification and
already as the beginning of the last judgment. Hope has a universal
breadth since the congregation can understand itself as the point in
time in salvation history in which God realizes his eternal salvific
resolution (cf. also Jas 5:8 f.).

The Letter to the Hebrews understands the revelation of the Son
(1:1–3) as the beginning of the eschatological phase of the salvation
historical self-revelation of God. The community of the faithful,
the Church, is the wandering people of God that within the power
of the salvation brought by Christ is on its way to its final goal
(10:34, 13:14). It is moving towards its already consummated (spatially) salvation on its way towards its anticipated consummation
(in time). In the face of the lapse in faith and the tepid character of
liturgical practice (6:1–8, 10:25) what counts is to look to Jesus, the
leader and perfecter of faith (12:2). Considering him precludes the
tiredness and the resignation in the competition which must be
withstood (12:1, 12:3.): "You need endurance to do the will of God
and receive what he has promised" (10:36).

The most recent NT scripture knows the Parousia delay as an occasion for skepticism. The mockers ask: "Where is the promise of his coming? From the time when our ancestors fell asleep, everything has remained as it was from the beginning of creation" (2 Petr 3:4). The author answers by pointing to God's loyalty and how God, for whom "a thousand years is like one day" and vice versa, has a different relationship to time (2 Petr 3:8; Ps 90:4). The Lord does not delay the fulfillment of his promises. But he is patient so that all have the opportunity to repent. The day of the Lord will come like a thief. That is why everyone should conduct themselves in holiness and devotion, waiting for and, as it were, "hastening" the coming of the day of God. After the expiration of the world God makes his promise come true and creates a "new heaven and a new earth" (Isa 65:17, 66:22; Rev 21:1; 2 Pet 3:13), in which all God's righteousness will dwell.

## f) The Eschatological Dimension in John

Jesus is the eternal Word that was with God and is God (John 1:1) and, in becoming flesh, has revealed the glory of the divinity. In his human life Jesus reveals himself as light and life, as truth and as the way to the Father. In his death and his glorification in the resurrection he proceeds all others to prepare a place for believers "in the house of his Father" (John 14:1 ff.).

For John, what stands in the foreground is the presence of salvation. The eschatological separation occurs here and now through the faith or lack of faith in the hearts of men. The Father and Son have made their dwelling place in believing and loving individuals, and the Spirit of God acts in them (John 14:23, 14:26). But the final revelation and consummation occurs when Christ returns. He will then gather the disciples so that they are there in the presence of the Father, where the Son also is (John 14:1–3, 16:16–33). This future dimension of the fulfillment of the eschatology in John strains somewhat but does not contradict eschatology of the present, as long as it is not reduced to existential Christology. "Who-

ever...believes...has eternal life" (John 5:24 and passim). But the
hour is coming in which the dead in the graves will also hear the
voice of the Son of God (John 5:25–28). Perhaps the insertion of
the words pertaining to "being raised on the last day" (John 6:39)
is meant to correct a docetic or gnostic misunderstanding of John
5:24, according to which all those who see the Son and believe in
him already have eternal life and that "whoever hears my word and
believes" has already "passed from death to life".

The struggle against the docetic deniers of the true humanity
of Jesus runs through the 1st and 2nd Letter of John (1 John 4:2).
This denial is a sign of the final days (1 John 2:18), in which the
Antichrist appears with his false doctrine (1 John 2:18, 2:23, 4:3; 2
John 7; cf. 2 Thess 2:2–4; Rev 13). What is important is the idea of
"remaining" of the communion of the Father and the Son and in
the fellowship (*koinonia*) of the brothers. Christological profession
of faith and brotherly love in action is what distinguishes the true
and false Christians in the Church. The consummation consists in
the likeness with God when we see him as he is (1 John 3:2). Seeing
God face to face (1 Cor 13:12) and the participation in the *koinonia*
of the love of Father, Son and Holy Spirit are the most vital statements of the Christian doctrine of consummation.

## g) The Revelation

This one apocalyptic book of the NT is not about the prediction
of cosmic events but about the interpretation of historic events and
the relationship with God in Christ. The apocalyptic images serve
to illustrate the salvific drama in the soul of the individual persons
and in history's major conflicts.

God is the Lord of History. In Christ the victory is achieved
over the powers hostile to God (Rev 1:5, 1:13–20). In the heavenly
liturgy of heavenly Jerusalem, the final victory is already celebrated.
In the consciousness of their unity with the church triumphant
the pilgriming and persecuted earthly Church can find consolation
and hope. At the climax of the salvific drama (Rev 12) God's last

opponents, the dragon, the beast, the false prophet and the whore Babylon re-appear and cast a spell over many people through blinding successes of earthly power and worldly wealth. After the visionary has seen the downfall of Babylon and the building of the new heaven and the new earth, in which death has been destroyed forever, he sees the time of a one-thousand year reign of the Messiah (Rev 20:1–6). What is meant is not a chronologically verifiable historical epoch. It is the kingdom of Christ and his Spirit over his disciples who, in the midst of affliction, persecution and martyrdom, profess their faith in him as the Lord. Christ's reign stands in the midst of the onslaught of these enemies as the unconquerable creative power at the side of those who follow the Lamb wherever he goes (Rev 14:5). It is the hidden presence of the kingdom of God in the Church that, together with the Spirit, supplicates for the coming of its bridegroom Jesus Christ (Rev 22:17) until its consummation at the wedding feast of the Lamb, for whom the Church has prepared herself as the bride (Rev 19:7, 19:9).

# III

# ASPECTS OF THE HISTORY OF THEOLOGY

## *1. Problems in Patristics*

### a) Eschatology and the Theology of History

The core content of eschatological statements of belief include the profession of faith in the return of Christ as the judge of both the living and the dead, the general resurrection of all men from the dead at the end of the world, the individual judgment after death and the general judgment in the last time as well as the consummation of the creation in the triune God, communion with God and eternal life.

Even if, in general, thought was guided by christologically focused eschatology, there were changes in perspective. For example, the dynamic understanding of time and history, as it predominated in semitic thinking, was frequently displaced by the more static juxtaposition of time and eternity, this life and the life in the hereafter.

Subsequent to the imminent expectation of the Parousia, the history between Pentecost and the second coming of Christ at the end of time became the theme of the Christian theology of history. Starting from the Christ event as the turn of the eon, the middle and fullness of time, periodizations resulted, punctuated by fixed theological dates such as the creation, the gift of grace, Adam's sin, the gift of the law, the fullness of grace in Christ and the final consummation (cf. the scheme: *ante legem, sub lege, sub gratia*).

Eusebius of Caesarea (265–339), in his work *Praeparatio evangelica*, compiles all the traces of the knowledge of God and morality in pre-Christian history which foreshadow the coming of Christ. Hence, he can see in pagan philosophy and its major figures a preparation for Christ wanted by God, comparable to the Old Testament as the preparation of the Jews for Christ.

In his major work of theological history, *De civitate Dei*, Augustinus (354–430) sees faith and disbelief or grace and sin as the two opposing motives whose conflict with each other drives the movement of history forwards. It is only in Christ that the atheism, amorality and blindness of paganism is overcome. But the underlying conflict remains and even intensifies, although, in the end, the victory of the *civitas Dei* over the *civitas terrena* shall come to pass.

## b) The Tension between Individual and Universal Eschatology (intermediate state)

Into the Middle Ages (e.g., Bernard of Clairvaux) universal eschatology remained the guiding point of reference. A consummation of the individual without his unity with the congregation was unthinkable. Nevertheless, the question arose concerning the status of those who die in the faith *prior to* the general end of the general resurrection (*status intermedius*). Based on the understanding of death as the separation of soul and body, the dominating thought was that man, centered in his soul, appears before God's judgment seat immediately following his death. It is there where man receives the judgment regarding his eternal destiny, the reward for good and the punishment for evil. In this intermediate state the soul waits in Sheol. But it already anticipates the final condition of the eternal blessing in heaven (especially the martyrs are already in communion with Christ) or, as well, the eternal punishment in hell. At the final judgment, at the time of the Parousia of Christ, the particular judgment is ratified. Through the resurrection of the body, man is completely restored, partakes in eternal life and is included in the communion of saints.

The problematic of the intermediate state is linked to the inclusion and essentially Christian transformation of the Greek teaching of immortality of the soul. Initially, the doctrine of the immortality of the soul was rejected because the soul in Greek philosophy was understood as something substantially divine, which not only contradicted the Christian conviction of its creatureliness, but also rendered superfluous God's commanding act of the resurrection of body and soul. The philosophers on the Areopagus in Athens scoffed at the proclamation of a resurrection of the dead (Acts 17:32). It was not possible to accept the soul into theology until it had been redefined: The soul as the created *principle of identity* of creaturely existence during its earthly life history, in the event of death and in the consummation of man in the life after death. The *indestructibility of the soul* is now the central Christian principle of the created human nature that forms the precondition for the reception of the supernatural salvific deed of the self-mediation of God in the awakening of Jesus. The body is reconstituted and consummated as the expression of the soul when, at the end of history, the whole of creation, including its material dimension, is renewed and has become the place of the consummated communication of personal spirits.

This way of thinking clearly appears in the first monograph on the theme: *On the Resurrection of the Body* by Athenagoras of Athens (around AD 170–180 ). The reason for the resurrection is God's will that created man in his own image for a "perpetual duration" (res. 12). The resurrection means "a change for the better." The initial intention of the resurrection is not the judgement, but rather the realization of God's salvific will in the consummation of man's nature (ibid 14). A spiritual nature endowed with a free will that consists of body and soul can only continue to exist into eternity because God awakened it from the dead and imparted life to it so that man continues to exist in the vision of God and the joy of his presence (ibid. 15, 25).

Although man receives grace through his reasonable soul, it is not only the soul that is reconstituted by grace, but rather the whole of man, his body and soul together, for his destination in eternal life.

> But if there is only one final goal of the whole [person], then this final goal...can be found neither in this life, as long as men are on earth, nor when the soul is separated from the body, because after the dissolution and complete dispersion of the body, despite the continued existence of the soul, man, according to the character of his being, is not present as he must be, hence it is absolutely necessary that the final goal of men appears in a reconstitution which, in turn, consists of both parts of the existing being. (ibid. 25)

The traditional ideas of the place where the soul remains in an intermediate status were conclusively surpassed by a specific development in Western medieval theology by the declaration of Pope Benedict XII in the constitution *Benedictus Deus* (DH 1000 ff.).

> The souls of the deceased that have died in justifying grace participate directly and immediately in heavenly beatitude, while the souls of those whose shortcomings are less grave, after purification and cleansing, also participate in the full vision of God. The souls of those who die in mortal sin are subjected to the damnation which they themselves have chosen.
>
> At the end, at the time of the general judgment and the general resurrection, men are finally restored to their complete corporeity.

## c) Prayer for the Dead, Communion of Saints, Purification (purgatorial fire)

> The Catholic understanding of purgatorial fire says that, after the death of those baptized and deceased in justifying grace, if there are any remaining temporary sin punishments and venial sins, there is a final purification, which enables the full vision of God

> through the suffering imposed by God's merciful judgment (satis-
> passio). In this, the Church can officially and privately, through
> intercession, works of charity (alms) and the celebration of mass,
> support the process of expatiating suffering of the residual resis-
> tances to the unification with God (Tertullian, monog. 10,4; Au-
> gustine, De cura pro mort. ger. 1,3; enchir. 110).

The purifying fire doctrine is based on three biblically rooted experiences, specifically (1.) the unity of grace and penitence, (2.)
the Church as the communion of salvation and the saints (3.) the
distinction between individual and general eschatology (from the
eleventh century).

(1.) After death, man bears the responsibility for his deeds in God's
court of justice (2 Cor 5:10). Associated with this is the idea of a
postmortal purification (regarding the metaphor of fire (cf. Deut
4:24; Isa 66:15; Heb 12:29; Rev 1:14; Matt 5:26, 12:31 and 1 Cor 3:15,
the classic reference for the doctrine of purgatorial fire). The fathers
refer to "purifying fire" (Origen, or. 29,15 and passim; *Ambrose*, in
Ps. 36,26; *Lactantius*, inst. 7, 21, 7; *Augustine*, enchir. 69, and passim; *Caesarius of Arles*, serm. 104, 2ff.; *Gregory I*, dial. 4,39). From
the unity of grace and repentance arises the question, what occurs in the particular judgment with the deceased, who in case of
grave guilt (after baptism) receive in the ecclesiastical process of
penitence the full reconciliation with God but prior to their death
have not yet performed all the required penitential exercises (that
are really the sin-cleansing and "working off" part of penitence).
Important in this context is the difference between the *mortal sin*
(1 John 5:16), that excludes the soul from the kingdom of God (Gal
5:21; Matt 12:32), and the *venial sins*, that are overcome through
daily prayer for forgiveness and works of charity, as well as the difference between *sin* as a grave guilt, that can only be remitted by
baptism or ecclesiastical reconciliation, and the *consequences*, that
remain existent at the re-attainment of justifying grace and require

a strenuous effort. The expiation required for the consequences of sin were more generally understood in the West as *vindictive/penal* (in reference to Matt 5:26; cf. *Tertullian*, an. 58; *Cyprian*, ep. 55, 20), in the East more *medicinal/healing* (*Clement of Alex.*, protr. I, 8, 3; *Origen*, hom. in Num. 25, 6).

(2.) The *prayer for the deceased* arises spontaneously from a natural bond and from the Christian conviction that death does not completely end the ties between the members of God's people, and from the hope of an eschatological restoration of the congregation (cf. 2 Macc 12:45; Rom 14:8; Phil 3:21; 2 Cor 5:9; John 11:25). This spontaneous prayer is associated with the explicit prayer for the penitents. It is provided to help them to shorten their penitence and also to come to the aid of those who died prior to the completion of the ecclesiastical process of penitence. Only since the thirteenth century can it be proven that an indulgence can also be allocated for the deceased.

(3.) In response to the question of the *status of the dead* ("intermediate state") the Church took up the Jewish Biblical ideas of the world beyond (Hades, paradise, heaven). Saints, souls in need of purification and the damned await the consummation of the final judgment. In the same vein, Pope Benedict XII explained in the constitution *Benedictus Deus* (1336): Every believer and baptized person who dies in the state of justifying grace "immediately" participates in the particular judgment in the beatifying vision of God and enters the communion of saints. Whoever dies without having repented mortal sin soon receives the judgment of damnation. Those who die in justifying grace, but still require purification of venial sins and temporary sin punishments, are not admitted into the vision of God until "after" a purification. At the end, all arise corporeally for the general judgment (DH 1000–02). At the ecumenical councils of Lyons (1274) and Florence (1439), for the first time, the Church magisterium referred to the existence of cleansing and purification punishments (*poenae purgatoriae seu catharte-rii*; DH 856; 1066; 1304). The terms *ignis purgatorius* or *purgatorium* are used less frequently because a spatial-temporal idea could take center stage (DH 1820; 1867; 2626).

The Orthodox churches see in this an allusion to the apocatasta-sis doctrine of Origen. The dogma does not include the "suffering" through a physical or spiritual fire (cf. 1 Cor 3:15: *"quasi" per ignem*). The "suffering" refers to the still unfulfilled attainment to the vision of God (*poena damni*) or the still unfulfilled inner consummation of the individual who has already been definitively saved (*poena sensus*).

The Reformers rejected the purgatory fire as "mera diaboli larva" (Luther, Smalcald Art. II, 2) or as "exitiale Satanae...commentum, quod Christi crucem evacuat" (J. Calvin, Inst. christ. rel. III, 5). The formal reason they give for this is the absence of any testimony in the scriptures; the substantial reason is the opinion that the doc-trine of purgatorial fire rests on justification through works; the mass for the deceased is a human sacrifice that casts doubt on the justification based *solely* on grace and faith or is intended to earn it through personal works for the performer of such works himself and for others. Today, what is important for the ecumenical dia-logue is that the Augsburg Confession includes a commemoration of the dead which takes the form of thanks to God and the prayer for the dead (Apologia Confessionis 24, 94 ff.).

The Council of Trent firmly insists on the existence of what is known as purgatory; the souls who are there, who died in justify-ing grace, but "have not yet been completely cleansed" (DH 1743; 1753), can be helped by intercession, alms and the celebration of Christ's Eucharistic sacrifice, that brought about propitiation for the living and the dead (DH 1820; 1866; 1487 ff.). All forms of superstition and indulgence abuse associated with purgatorial fire are denounced (DH 1820). The II Vatican Council reinforces the awareness of the unity of the Church in all its members, who are pilgriming to God, need cleansing after death or are already in the presence of full glory of God (LG 49 f.).

## 2. *The Resurrection Treatise in Scholastics*

In contrast to the more sporadic occupation of the Church Fathers, Scholasticism developed a systematic eschatology. There are detailed discussions about questions concerning the resurrection of soul and body, the identity of the resurrected body, the connection of the saints in heaven with the believers on earth sanctified in grace and the souls of the deceased in purgatorial fire, the question of the relationship of particular and general judgment, the type of beatitude (which, according to Thomas, is more in the beatifying vision of God, while Duns Scotus places greater emphasis on the unification in love with God), the question of the corporeity of the damned and their suffering, the difference between the *poena damni*, i.e., the loss of the supernatural communion with God and the *poena sensus*, i.e., the consequences of damnation and its appearance in the spiritual-corporeal being of man.

A pregnant summary of the Thomist conception of eschatology is contained in the *Summa contra gentiles* IV, 79–97.

### a) The Future Resurrection

Through Christ's crucifixion and resurrection men have been freed from Adam's sin and its consequence, eternal death. The effect of Christ's suffering is mediated by the sacraments. Baptism and, possibly, penitence, results in the forgiveness of sin. Man enters the supernatural relationship with God and, through the grace of the sacrament, receives a pledge of the future glory. Not until the end of the world do men receive the full effect of the resurrection, the overcoming of death as a punishment for sin, when Christ with his power awakens all the dead.

If reason cannot force the acceptance of the thought of the resurrection, still, this thought can be made apparent to reason if the point of departure of the argument is the being of man and the purpose of his existence. According to the intention of the creator, the soul was created immortal. It is the principle of the creaturely

existence of man. It realizes the spiritual-corporeal unity and describes the disposition of the spiritual and free nature of man for
the reception of supernatural grace. The soul is the continuous
bearer of the created nature of man in all its historical modalities.
The essence of the soul contradicts a being outside of the matter in
which it subsists. If in death through the decay of the body matter
is destroyed, the soul remains incomplete and it is in its nature to
demand the complete restoration of the body-soul integrity. But
because such a resurrection exceeds the soul's own strength, only
God himself can bring about the resurrection of man, i.e., both the
restoration of the integral nature of man as well as its consummation through grace. But man is not restored after his death from
nothingness by means of God's memory, so that between man in
his earthly existence and in his consummation in heaven there
would be no natural identity. In death only the connection of the
constitutive principles of individual soul and matter is detached.
But the soul remains the principle of identity and the substantial
form of the body-soul unity. Matter remains the possible basis into
which the soul brings the individuality and personality of man
and his subsistence. Hence, without a body, the soul never exists
completely because, as the substantial form, it guarantees the metaphysical identity of the self-expression in the matter and, hence, the
corporeal identity of man as well. In this sense, man arises in his
"own body" into eternal life and appears in material identity with
his earthly existence: *in numero idem*. What is to note here is that
soul and matter are active as metaphysical principles. There is no
empirical and quantifiable continuity that could be established by
man in *statu viatoris*. But if in death a member is absent, or if the
man was corporeally deformed from the beginning of his existence,
through the omnipotence and goodness of God, all shortcomings
are remedied, because in the redeemed and consummated matter
the consequences of sin are so completely overcome that the soul
imposes its necessary three-dimensional forming power on matter. Hence, the specific appearance of man can correspond to his
generic appearance.

## b) The Conditions of the Resurrected Bodies

The resurrection of Christ lays the foundation for the resurrection of all men at the end of the world as well as their natural and supernatural consummation. The incorruptibility of the resurrected men is rooted in their participation in God's eternity. It is not man as a genus that participates in God's eternity but rather every individual person. This is emphasized against the idea of a quasi-immortality in the sense that man is an endlessly reproducing genus while the individual falls victim to death. In the state of eternal consummation the difference between the sexes remains; it belongs to the integrity of the nature of the male and female body and is also an expression of the wisdom of the Creator, who arranges the order of creation in such a way that the variety of the finite reveals the eternal beauty of God. However, the eternal life does not consist in the enjoyment of meals for maintenance of individual life, meals that are not longer necessary. And, because of the end of history, there is no longer any need for procreation of offspring. God himself becomes the source and the epitome of all joy which fills the soul and finds its resonance in corporeal existence. The natural desire of man to see God (*desiderium naturale ad videndum Deum*) comes to fruition in love. Man indeed sees God directly, but in a creaturely way, mediated by the humanity of Jesus.

Man rises from the dead in his true body, not in an ethereal form. He has been afforded the dowry (*dotes*) through which the soul can more adequately accomplish its matrimonial unity with the life of God. The dowry of the soul are the *vision*, the *love* and the *pleasure* of God (*visio, dilectio, fruitio*). The corporeal blessings are: the freedom from suffering and the best possible adaptation of the body to the soul (*impassibilitas, subtilitas, agilitas, claritas*).

For the damned the situation is just the opposite. They also share in the corporeal resurrection of the body, because corporeity is a part of man's nature and is good. But they do not share in the grace which takes place as God's self-mediation in the resurrection of Christ. For the will of the individual man remains turned away from God. His soul is ruled by the total frustration of the *desiderium naturale*. The loss of the supernatural vision of God (*poena damni*) corresponds to the refused dowry of the body that is expressed in the disharmony (*poena sensus*) of body and soul and in the individual corporeal realizations of man (*affectus carnalis, corpus ponderosum et grave, passibilia opaca et tenebrosa*).

The saints differ from the damned in that their will is firmly anchored in the good that God is in himself and that he proclaims to the world. By contrast, the will of the damned is in contradiction with God, which is why a renewed conversion is impossible. The punishment of hell does not ensue from a decree handed down by God but rather is the final solidification of the freely chosen willful contradiction of the offer of grace. It cannot be reversed because God as the transcendent Goal of the will has been definitively missed.

## c) Death and Judgment

The soul, separated from the body at the time of death, has left its pilgrim status (*status viatoris*) behind: It can no longer earn rewards. After death, the soul comes immediately to its goal (*terminus*); whether it receives its reward in heaven or its punishment in hell. There are saved, who, despite the love through which they belong irreversibly to God, are still burdened with something which requires purification. For them there is a delaying moment in the attainment of the final goal. This is meant soteriologically, not chronologically. The faithful conviction of the Church in the existence of the purification process (purgatorial fire) has its sufficient basis in the custom of the Church to pray for the dead. But it would be senseless if there were no help for them from our prayer, because prayer for the saints is superfluous and senseless for the damned. Even before the final judgment the saints live in a full vision of God. In terms of its *intensity* it cannot be magnified. Yet through the complete unification with its body, i.e., its expression in the renewed matter of the newly created heaven, the new earth and the full communion of saints, it obtains its *extensive* cumulation.

At the final judgment, the final form of the creation shall be prepared. What occurs in man is the consummation of his natural desire for a vision of God. It is through the resurrection of Christ that man has been endowed with grace. It is evident and fully realized in the life of the new world.

IV

# SYSTEMATIC PRESENTATION
# OF THE ESCHATOLOGY

The systematic presentation of the eschatology must proceed theocentrically because God himself is the leader and perfecter of his creation. From Revelation we know God, the Father, the Son and the Spirit as *love* in himself and towards us. In relation to the world he remains the measure of the creation, especially its personal center, man. In this way God reveals himself as *righteousness*. If the creature in the interactive-historical encounter with God and in the shaping of his life meets his designated purpose in spirit and freedom by participating in the essence and form of the Son of God made man in the Holy Spirit (Rom 8:29), then God encounters him as *life*, i.e., as the fulfillment of his striving for sense and being. Thus, we have a triune theocentrical aspect for the systematic eschatology: 1. God is love: the Father, 2. God is righteousness: the Son, 3. God is eternal life: the Spirit.

## *1. God Is Love: The Reign of the Father*

(1.) *In his essence*: In his historical self-revelation we can see that God not only loves the world, but rather that in his essence itself is love. His essence is accomplished as the eternal origin of love in the Father, as the eternal self-encounter in his self-expression in the Word (Son). In this sense the Son is eternally grateful in his divinity. Father and Son are found as love, that in turn is identical with God's essence through which God subsists, in the Holy Spirit. Thus, in God all is God as love.

(2.) *Regarding the creation*: The personality of man through which he, and the whole of creation with him, enters into a conversational partnership with God, is unnecessary for God's own fulfillment. But if God wants the creation he also endows it with such structures through which it can transcend itself towards him. Hence, if the created personality is the partner in bearing the transcendent meaning of creation, it includes reason (= from and through the word, ability to communicate) and will. Through reason the created person can participate in God's self-knowledge in the Word (Son), through will, in God's self-affirmation in the Spirit. Hence, every created person is made to attain to the knowledge and the love of God. Inherent to his created nature is an analogous relationship to God as the origin and, hence, to the Father, a God-centricity in the Son, and a relationship to God as the goal in the participation in the self-determination to himself in the Holy Spirit. Hence, God is the origin, the middle and the goal of the creature endowed with mind and freedom. So part of human nature is a history of freedom through which it either arrives at God's original self-offering or misses it.

The doctrine of belief says that man rejected the offer originally meant for him and, hence, missed God himself in his self-transcendence in reason and will. Although this meant that he lost the communion with God in knowledge and love, nevertheless, his natural orientation towards God, i.e., his religious-ethical facility and his transcendent relationship remains; however, he can no longer activate it himself. Hence, due to sin, an enormous rift runs through all of creation. Sin is the contradiction to God's salvific will and the contradiction of man to his essence and goal. This rift through the middle of creation, that is conditioned by the rejection of its self-transcendence towards the God of love from which it proceeds and towards whom it is moving, can only be healed by God. Closing this breach is only possible when God himself, incarnate, enters into creation and brings about its self-transcendence from creaturely existence to its goal.

**(3.)** *In its salvation historical self-unfolding*: This new salvific will towards the goal of an incarnation of God (John 1:14, 3:16), that is oriented towards reconciliation and a new relationship to man in beatifying grace, can only be accomplished corresponding to the historical structure of human freedom in the form a salvation history that from the first promises of blessing to Abraham and the history of the covenant in the Old Testament leads to "the fullness of time" in which God himself realizes himself in a human nature. It is in this human form assumed by God that the new founda-tion of the creation takes place. Its transcendentality towards God, which was abrogated by sin, recovers its original realization—in this consists the essence of the forgiveness of sins—and it rises in-deed to God in the grace of eternal life.

Because of the necessary unity of divine self-mediation and its as-sumption of creaturely existence born by the Logos itself, it is also understood why only the Logos itself could assume human nature. Through his personal and unrelinquishable acceptance by human-ity, itself born by the Logos, Jesus Christ is therefore also the head of the new humanity and its steadfast mediator to the threefold God. Redemption, forgiveness of sins and the new covenant with God are mediated by him so that we become members of Christ's body. We enter with him, in the reality of grace and morally disposed, into a community of life in which we become his brothers and sisters. The incarnation of God finds its most extreme historical expression in the cross of Jesus. In this expression, the self-contradiction of the creation is overcome from within in divine grace and creaturely devotion.

What counts then, in a renewed creation, reopened towards God, is to know and love God. But the new knowledge of God is mediated by the Son. "Now this is eternal life, that they should know you, the only true God, and the one whom you sent, Jesus Christ" (John 17:3). The new love of God, through which we are one with the threefold God, to the extent that he lives in us and we are pilgriming towards him as our goal, is born by the Holy Spirit that has been given to us in our hearts (= will) (Rom 5:5). That is why the outpouring of the Holy Spirit over the *whole* of humanity belongs to the inner-historical closure of the revelation of the Son in human nature.

(4.) *In regards to the consummation of man*: That the final fulfillment of man's being is in communion with God can only be recognized if we participate in the history of God's self-revelation in faith. God revealed himself in his innermost, essential being as threefold love, and every spiritual and free creature is called upon to participate in their realization in knowledge and love. This is the metaphysical salvation historical meaning of the sentence: "God is love" (1 John 4:8, 4:16b).

## 2. God Is Our Righteousness: The Reign of the Son

### a) The trinitarian God as the measure of the creature

All the basic statements about God in Christian theology are trinitarian, incarnational and pneumatological. Man is governed by a dialogic relationship with God which is integral to him as a creature and which was given again to him, the sinner, in the redemption and the sanctification through the gift of the Holy Spirit. All this plainly sets out the limits of a merely moral or deistic divine relationship.

In light of the trinity mystery, grace is endowment of participation in life, through which God enables the creatures oriented towards him to activate their self-transcendence in spirit and freedom. In this way, the path is reopened for the creatures with an inner disposition and outer way of life in harmony with God to come to him and be consummated in the beatifying communication with him in his eternal and incarnational love. In this sense, the "judgment of man" is a "justification" in the sense of "being made just" so that man in his disposition and action—to the extent that they are the expression of this love—can correspond to the loving

God and receives his beatification as being fulfilled with God's holiness. In a unity of knowledge and will with God, he knows the Father through, with and in the Son in unity of love in the Holy Spirit, that causes our will to reflect the will with which the Father wants the Son, and the Son, knowing himself to be wanted forever by the Father, in gratitude, himself wants to be oriented towards the Father.

## b) "Christ, who became for us ... righteousness, sanctification, and redemption" (1 Cor 1:30)

In Christ, the righteousness through which God makes us just (*iustitia Dei passiva*) has become historical reality. By becoming man through the assumption of human nature the Son, in the divine grace with which he unifies (*gratia unionis*), also already encompasses the grace through which he, as the head of the new humanity (*gratia Christi capitis*), includes all men in the renewed human nature, his body, and opens the way to communion with God. In this way, Christ, who was made for us for the sake of righteousness in the incarnation, can also be our righteousness.

For the new righteousness, founded in the incarnation, originating from God in Christ, to which we adhere to embrace God, has its goal in the cross and the resurrection of Jesus.

Seen from the humanity of Jesus, his complete obedience corresponds to the righteousness given to us in him through which we are in the likeness of God. The complete subjugation of his human will to divine will—"Thy will be done" (Luke 22:42)—lead him in the obedient loyalty to his mission unto death on the cross (Phil 2:8). But that is also why he was raised by God to sit at his right hand in the glory of the Father (Eph 1:20). In his name, all Gentiles should now be led "to the obedience of faith" (Rom 1:5). Someone who is justified by faith, i.e. who corresponds to the righteousness and holiness of God in Jesus Christ, will live.

Jesus was crucified because "Jews and Gentiles"—through our disobedience—did not accept the righteousness assured in him:

"For God delivered all to disobedience, that he might have mercy on all" (Rom 11:32). Yet it is specifically in this way that God proves his righteousness to be a mercy made evident, that he reveals in the obedience maintained by Jesus unto the death on the cross the message now finally accepted by man of his self as the communion of love. In the cross and in the remaining scars of the transfigured body of the resurrected the theocentricity of the world interpreted christologically becomes irrevocable: "For from him and through him and for him are all things" (Rom 11:36). If we in our obedience become like Jesus in his will to devotion, God's righteousness is our portion. Then we are justified: "Whoever believes in him will not be condemned" (John 3:18).

## c) Theological Treatment of Death

### Death as the "wages of sin"

Death should not be merely looked at biologically, but theologically as well. Death is the manifestation of our abandonment by God. That is why we experience it as an obliterating and paralyzing force, as the radical isolation from love, from transcendental meaning and as fear of nihility in the sense that nihility "is" the complete absence of life and love. In death begins the experience of forsakenness; the trembling before death is the shadow of hell, i.e., of the irreversible loss of an opportunity to transcend the material universe and approach God, who originates and provides the fullness which determines the goal. This is the death that Jesus took upon himself as a substitute. Although he himself stood "without sin" in the most intimate communion with the Father, he "bore the punishment that makes us whole" (Isa 53:5). Yes, "For our sake he made him to be sin who did not know sin, so that we might become the righteousness of God in him" (2 Cor 5:21). Through the death of Christ, our death has the dual character of the judgment on God-forsakenness, on the one hand, and the free devotion to God's far greater love for us implanted in the death of Christ. What occurs in baptism *in mysterio* and as sacramental burial with Christ, and what the faithful knows in the resurrection of Christ himself as revelation of the glory of the Father, that is ratified in our real death and brought into a final form. "For if we have grown into union with him through a death like his, we shall also be united with him in the resurrection" (Rom 6:5; cf. Phil 3:10). Having become one forever in the love with God in complete correspondence, i.e., in true "holiness and righteousness" (Luke 1:75; Eph 4:24), we look from God back on our real death and know in him our transformation into the finality of what had begun in baptism and in faith, was proven in hope and which has matured in love.

Whatever good has been done in the name of Jesus will not pass away, but rather, in a transformed, inwardly refined form, enter into the eternal: "Blessed are the dead who die in the Lord from now on; let them find rest from their labors, for their works accompany them" (cf. Rev 14:13; Heb 4:10). The consummated Kingdom of God is not an abstract eternity in which the earthly, historical and the work of man's hand descends into non-existence. In the resurrected world of the new earth and the new heaven this is the ἀποκατάστασις πάντων (Acts 3:21), the universal restoration.

## The status of the dead

It is theologically inappropriate to describe death merely naturally and biologically or to define it using the vague formula "separation of soul and body," only then to question the location and state of the soul after death and to philosophize about its temporal relationship to the corporeal resurrection. Instead, in the center of the Christian eschatology are the soteriological statements. This does not involve anticipated descriptions of the kind found in a feature article but rather the soteriologically defined relation to God of the person of whom we believe and know that he in death has entered into a final relationship to God. Just for the purpose of securing this term we shall devote some time to the natural side of death.

Anthropologically we do not understand man as being composed of an already made soul and an already made body. As a substantial union of body and soul he is established in a subsistent act of being expressed in the one and whole matter of creation, taking form as this empirical man in the here and there of his being-in-the-world (*anima forma corporis*). In his inner self man is in spirit unlimitedly open to being, and in his will to the freely chosen relationship to what is good is so self-mediated that the soul of man is ontologically determined by a three-way relation:

1. through the transcendental relation to God;
2. through its relationship to itself in self-understanding and in self-determination;
3. through its relationship to the world, i.e., both in the individual sense as well as in a broader social and historical sense, the relationship to the world as the basis of the person's potential, his surroundings, from which the soul receives the potential wealth of the realization of its essence.

In death the order of importance of these three basic relations changes. Because of the meaning of creation that is manifest in man as a subsistentially spiritual act of being, death cannot be annihilation, otherwise the dynamic of the creation would not lead to God but to nothingness. In death, man, taking into account his transcendental relation to God, enters into a final relationship to the resurrected Christ in the Holy Spirit. The natural basis of the supernatural consummation in grace is the created hypostasis/person of man who bears the spiritual and corporeal composite of human nature.

In relation to himself he is in the status of certainty and joy in his salvation.

In relation to the world, whose empirical dimension—from the viewpoint of those left behind—he has departed, he is in a natural, transcendental relationship, in relation to men, in the soteriological relationship of solidarity in salvation. For his will conforms to the will of God, whose purpose is always the salvation of men; that is why there can exist a reciprocal knowledge in intercession and petition relative to prayer between the saints in heaven and the faithful. In the vision of God mediated by the Logos they see our world. They themselves are not immaterial because the redeemed world has also entered into the form of its consummation. But through the openness of continuing world history, they are related to the transformation brought about at Christ's Parousia, including the transformation of matter into a new earth and a new heaven. It is from this consummated matter and not, say, from matter created *ad hoc ex nihilo* somewhere beyond the created world, that they take on their respective consummated corporeity in the full sense.

### Time, death and eternity

There is no chronological and spatial extension in the sense as they now constitute the decaying and dissipating in the world of experience that places itself so awkwardly as an obstacle in the way of personal integration. But a creature can never be so completely identical with his actual self-realization as God whose eternity is nothing other than his being. Man consists of form *and* matter, whose inherently diverse ways of realization are integral to his own being. But by realizing his potentials he is capable of coming into his own, so that instead of losing himself in the process of collecting and ordering their diversity he comes through them into the whole wealth of his personality lightly and easily. In this sense, analogously, one can also call the new way of being of the man, transfigured in mind and body, eternal (*totum et simul*). It is the prerequisite for a participation in God's eternal life, that is only already eternal through his being, for God *nullo modo compositus est, sed est omnino simplex* (Thomas v. A., S. th. I q. 3 a. 7). The man who is consummated in the communion with God has not yet shed his history and being-in-the-world. After all, he brought it into his immediate presence before the one who will be his God forever and ever.

### Postmortal judgment and the purification (purgatorial fire)

According to biblical testimony, the "judgment" is after death: "We must all appear before the judgment seat of Christ, so that each one may receive recompense, according to what he did in the body, whether good or evil" (2 Cor 5:10).

To come to a proper understanding it is necessary to overcome a cosmically, physically and chronologically hypostatized image. Our relationship to God is primary. In this regard, we believe that, in our death, it receives its final, christologically constituted form. Then our death means coming into the final all-encompassing embrace of Jesus Christ, the embodiment of righteousness, God made man. By standing up for us he has made it possible for us to approach God. It is provided to us in grace, must be assumed by us in faith and must also be accepted in love. The love through which we are empowered in the Holy Spirit to accept into ourselves the living communion with God offered eschatologically and irreversibly in Christ is the actual form of existence that is formed in our outer activity in life. In this way, the unity with God in love proves itself as the determining gauge measure against which we are measured. Hence, postmortal judgment is something altogether different than a balancing of accounts in the world to come. Instead, it is the determination of whether we, in love, as it has taken form in our "work," correspond to the sacred God in the same form as Christ, who we know as our righteousness before God. In this way, Christ, as judge (Matt 25:31 ff.) of the resurrected on the last day, will call in the works of corporeal charity. This spiritual gift is in the fruit of the spirit that Paulus sees expressed in love, joy, peace, etc. (Gal 5:22). Finally, this is nothing other than the likeness of Christ accepted into our way of life and the full acceptance of Christ's righteousness in the inner man and its full correspondence in the outer man. In other words, the postmortal judgment is the realization of the final mediation of God's love for us, through which he, from within, penetrates the plurality of our finite self-realizations so thoroughly that our consummated existence is nothing but a pure, complete and blessed togetherness with Christ, the God made man, in the Holy Spirit towards the Father from whom all inner-divine and created being has its origin and in which it finds its goal in the *communio* of divine love (cf. 2 Cor 13:13). From our side, judgment means the last acceptance of our being accepted through our whole life from its integrating middle (the soul) and into its form (body): *Judgment is the acceptance, become definitive in death, of our being accepted in Jesus, the Christ* (cf. 1 John 4:13–21).

## Purification in judgment

Prior to passing on to complete and blessed correspondance with God, there remains the purification process, the purgatorium, the cleansing punishment, a test in God's fire of love.

At judgment, God reconciles man completely with himself to become a consummated holistic form. The image "fire" (1 Cor 3:15), that biblically often is used in connection with the words of judgment, means the love of God in its testing, purifying and refining violence. The person sitting in judgment can withstand this because, through his final affiliation with Christ's righteousness, this encounter is only experienced as unification in love. But the pain inherent in this encounter holds sway in the experience of any love, when it receives more love than it is able to return through its own purity and fullness, from which, through negligence, it has fallen away. The soul passes through the pain of this difference in the form of the *passio* in order to be able to accomplish this love in the full sense as a free *actio* of self-devotion. Its knowledge that it is only capable of this through the free and empowering instruction of the loved one gives the form of its love the moment of gratitude and confession that is all grace and that our ability to love continues to have its precondition in being loved by God.

## Particular and general judgment

The discussion of postmortal judgment would not be complete without addressing how it relates to and differs from the general judgment on the last day. Are there two judgments involved here?

In the critical dismissal of two important theological mediation attempts, for one, the idea of the separation of body and soul with an immediate beatitude of the soul and a later judgment via the body, and, for another, the conception of the soul's sleep that is based on the merging of eternity and the moment of death, eschatology must be oriented solely with respect to the soteriological standard of the profession of faith, that the judgment has an individual and a communal dimension. In his death, the individual person finally encounters the God of love in Christ with whom all the saints are already joined, specifically as an individual in his whole undelegable freedom and unique personality. But he encounters God in the social constitution, inherent to his essence, that is inserted into the whole network of human history in salvation and downfall. This is the judgment as the universal and human event. Hence, it is not so much a temporal as it is a soteriological coincidence of particular and general judgment that must be accepted in the sense that man himself is always only an individual in the realization of his social relation to the whole of humanity and its history. This totality will find its consummation and be revealed in Christ when the Son hands over the kingdom to the Father so that God reigns over everything and may be all in all (1 Cor 15:28), and Christ may be all in all (Col 3:11).

### *The irreversible acceptance of being accepted: heaven*

> Heaven is the accepted self-mediation of God or the fulfillment in grace of the desiderium naturale ad videndum Deum in the mode of unlosableness.

Outside of God, man cannot find the goal that it is in his nature, i.e., in his creaturely being, to journey towards the later unburdened enjoyment of intellectual and sensual joys. His goal is God himself and heaven is the kingdom of God that has come completely to us. In heaven he meets God himself as the content of his beatitude, his eternal happiness and never-ceasing joy. And in God he also finds himself in the communion of all the saved. The accomplishment of the communion of saints is not something he experiences as a superficial add-on, say, as a secondary source of beatitude. God is the one source of all encompassing and fulfilling love that also flows like a river through the social relations between the saints. Hence, charity is not an ingredient added to the love of God but its embodiment oriented towards the co-redeemed. The communion of saints does not stand in contradiction to the theocentricity and Christocentricity of the creation in its redeemed form. Each saint is only recognized in God, and each love of him knows itself be coming from and born by God and directed towards him as well. Then, God does not see the loved person as a competitor. He need not be afraid that something is lost to him. God himself honors his servants: "The Father will honor whoever serves me" (John 12:26). God requires no honor from his creatures. He honors himself in his deeds: the creation and the redemption. "For the glory of God is a living man; and the life of man consists in beholding God" (Irenaeus of Lyons, haer. IV, 20, 7).

This thought also underlies the Christian honoring of the saints. They are not additional centers or recipients of piety beside God or beside Christ. In them the believer honors on earth the power of God's transforming grace. Every expression of respect towards them, especially the recognition of their exemplary lives, means God's honor in them (DH 675). And their intercession, which we are permitted to to request from them, also presumes that all of God's grace and his help in daily life comes from only him, but that he associates some of his gifts with the intercessory prayer of the saints to make clear the social-communal dimension of salvation.

The prayer of the faithful is always directed towards the Father through the Son in the Holy Spirit. But Christ stands by us in a dual sense. As the head of the Church he is the origin of all grace and the originating mediator of our prayer to the Father. But Christ is also present in the Church, his body. Each act of the members for each other, including prayer in particular, is an expression of Christ's presence for others. What is expressed in prayer for each other is being together in faith and in love. The call upon the saints in heaven thus means setting oneself in relation to the we of the ecclesiastical congregation of prayer that, in the Resurrected, reaches beyond the limit of death in order to arrive in, with and through Christ as an individual among the members of Christ's body in the presence of the Father, so that we, in complete obedience, which we have recognized in Christ, open ourselves to his will, that is identical with our salvation. Hence, the Christian honoring of the saints is one of the central aspects of the ecclesiastical eschatology (cf. LG ch. VII, No. 48–51).

Heaven means participation in the life of the threefold God. In and with the incarnated Son we know God, as he is, in the vision of his essentiality, that subsists in the three divine persons. We let our will be moved to participate in the communion of love between the Father and Son in the Holy Spirit that has been given to us (Rom 5:5).

However, do we avail ourselves of the secret of the threefold God through our complete knowledge of God, that transforms faith into vision and hope into the experience of the presence of salvation, and through our complete and liberated love of God?

Here we must allow for the structure of our finite knowledge that, of course, in terms of its nature remains finite and creaturely, even if it was uplifted in the Logos and the Holy Spirit beyond itself to an activity which, on its own, it would not be capable of. In his revelation God showed himself. After our death he will no longer be accepted and believed by means of creaturely knowledge images but rather he will show himself to us in his essentiality through which we will know him and, hence, by way of looking, i.e., unmediated awareness of his presence. But the limitation resides in how we, nevertheless, do not know God in a divine way, but rather in our creaturely way. Thus, we comprehend God indeed as the object of our vision, but even as the unfathomable depth of his trinitarian person-reality.

So, our vision of God may always be at its goal, but in such a way that his present is at the same time his future, as a dynamic and beatifying, unfathomable, mysterious Destination. If now, however, creaturely reality is and remains incarnationally marked by God's incarnation, so must we also profess that the human nature of the

Logos into which we are poured through the grace of participation, remains eternally the medium and the tendency of man towards the threefold God.

### *The objection to being accepted in Christ: hell*

Just as heaven is not a fairy-tale land of abundance, hell is not a torture chamber in the world beyond where the revenge of a rejected lover rages in all kinds of cruelty and brutality intensified even more by the hopelessness of ever escaping this place of torment.

This is how Christian theology imagined the magisterially defined doctrine of the eternity of infernal punishment as a true crux of the proclamation. At this point glad tidings appeared to turn into threatening tidings. That is why eminent theologians (Origen, Gregory of Nyssa) gave consideration to the doctrine of an all-encompassing reconciliation including the acceptance of a conversion which also included demons and the damned after a longer punishment of purification. Christianity among the members of the bourgeoisie, as it has evolved under the influence of the enlightenment, resisted the doctrine of the eternity of hell for other reasons. In this context, the relation between God and man is understood merely morally. Grace only appears as a kind of generosity on the part of God. Mercifulness, on the other hand, is, so to speak, the equivalent of closing both eyes, a superior point of view from which it is clear that man's actions cannot be taken altogether seriously.

Against this stands the unambiguous doctrine of the Bible. This refers not only to the statements of the unquenched fires of hell and the eternal removal from the communion of God, but also to the basic statements about the freedom of the creature and the character of grace as a dialogic process of the unification in love, to which the duality of self-mediation and assumption belongs. Most importantly, a strictly moralistic argument must be avoided just as much as are pseudo-speculations about a balance of the two abstractly considered characteristics of God's righteousness and mercifulness.

Every statement about hell is hermeneutically within the framework of soteriology. Christ is the revealed righteousness of God.

God's righteousness in Christ *is* his mercifulness and his mercifulness consists in the fact that he has made us righteous through the redemption in Christ. His revelation is nothing less than the realization given in Christ of his general salvific will (1 Tim 2:4). He assumed his historical form in Christ as arrived and assumed self-giving in the communion of love. On his way to the cross and in his descent into the realm of the dead, Christ completely undid man's distance from God (the *poena damni*). He himself, the communion with him, becomes the criterion of whether we will ever accept the assumption of all of humanity individually for us as well. Since Christ, damnation does not mean that God is lacking in mercifulness. All guilt, for no matter what sins, has already been overcome. There is no guilt that is not already forgiven in Christ. Even the most brutal crimes are included into forgiveness for in Christ's cross they are stripped of their culpable character. He bore everything to the cross and has atoned for *all* sin. Therefore, in hell, there is no unatoned sin. God's grace and mercifulness is not absent there. Instead, and in this consists the paradox of all paradoxes, this mercifulness is rejected as an expression of self-perverting freedom.

There is no hell as such in a parallel sense as there is a heaven. It is the self-mediation attained in Christ that, in this mode of rejection, clings to the individual person. It is the error and delusion of non-acceptance of being accepted.

In discussing any act performed freely and responsibly by a personal mind, a distinction must be drawn between the principle from which it is done, for one, and, for another, the outer form of the deed itself. Christ overwhelmed all evil to the extent that it was the expression of a weak, perverted will, and made possible a new form through the outwards realization of love towards God and towards our fellow man. But this will cannot be forced. If the influence went beyond an urgent invitation, the result would be the nullification not only of free will but also of the self-transcendence towards goodness for its own sake and to the God in Jesus Christ. The result would be the logically and really impossible coexistence of compulsion and love. However, love can only be the self-expression of freedom. That is why all events involving sin and crime can be forgiven and overcome. Man is granted the forgiving grace of a new communion of love through and beyond his outward deeds if in remorse as the first expression of love he transcends his will and his inner disposition to the acceptance of his assumption. But this will must be and remain absolutely free for the sake of the greater good of the communion of love with God. But this refers to the sin against the Holy Spirit:

> Therefore, I say to you, every sin and blasphemy will be forgiven people, but blasphemy against the Spirit will not be forgiven. And whoever speaks a word against the Son of Man will be forgiven; but whoever speaks against the holy Spirit will not be forgiven, either in this age or in the age to come. (Matt 12:31–32)

This does not concern a specific matter of sin. What is involved is the refused self-transcendence towards the God of love caused by a specific form of rejection of the new form of our will, with which we are endowed in the Holy Spirit and through which we are united with God in eternal life.

But then, the coherence between the inner form of will and tangible deeds is only transparent for God. Even radically evil behavior regarding matter need not be the adequate expression of a radically evil will. That is why there is hope for everyone for a spark of love which God can arouse into a fire.

The doctrine of the church of hell is limited under the standard of soteriology to two moments:

1) The contradiction of a definitive type, ratified in death, against God's self-mediation revealed in Christ as love and man's goal is *really possible*.

2) *Who, how many* and *if any* men have continued to put up a radical resistance to love unto the moment of death, is unknown to us not merely by chance, but as a matter of principle. But we should hope and pray that God's general salvific will extended to every man will achieve its goal for all men. There may still be God's love and accepted self-mediation where God and Christ are not explicitly known. That is why those who have fed the hungry as a charitable deed that they come to stand on the right side of the judge. "When did we see you hungry and feed you, or thirsty and give you drink?" (Matt 25:37); "[Amen, I say to you,] whatever you did for one of these least brothers of mine, you did for me" (Matt 25:40). And these will go as "righteous" to eternal life (Matt 25:46).

In Christ there is, thus, only one outcome of history, although mention of the real possibility of the accursed departing "into the eternal fire prepared for the devil and his angels" (Matt 25:41), initially, suggests, as a literary composition, a dualistic outcome. In Christ humanity has definitively come to God, its sole goal, although a few may also stubbornly persist in rejecting God. A concrete image of such a manner of existence is completely closed to us. The only thing possible is the view into the abyss of created freedom in order to either fathom the beatitude of its consummation in the love of God or to flinch at its failure.

### 3. God Is Eternal Life: The Koinonia in the Spirit of the Father and the Son

We had looked at systematic eschatology first in terms of how God is inherently the love which is historically communicated in the acts of creation, forgiveness, redemption and sanctification. In adddition, a further aspect was that God made man like himself by making Christ the sole decisive form in which we satisfy God, through the incarnation of the Logos, through its proclamation of the Kingdom of God and through its consommate realization in the cross, resurrection and exaltation.

Then, after our perception of God as the *origin* and God as *the way and goal*, there is, third, our perception of God as the *substance of human fulfillment*. Hence, faith, summarizing all the stations of its profession, looks to the "eternal life," the life in the future world (cf. Apostolicum and Nicaeno-Constantinopolitanum).

### a) What Is Eternal Life?

"In him [God] we live and move and have our being" (Acts 17:28). *Eternal life is our consummated fulfilling communion with God.*

That is why the final form of our being is called "life" because it is not only a matter of purely factual existence in the way that a stone exists. "Life" means that inner determination of a being that makes possible an inwardness in relation to itself, self-possession, and free behavior towards another. In the highest sense, life is adapted to person. Through the two fundamental activities of the mind, the activity of reason and will, man achieves his goal in communion with God. The active participation in God's absolute activity, insofar as God is pure, acting reality (*actus purus*), means a fulfilled life in the broadest sense conceivable. This life is then termed eternal. Here we must ask how eternity and time should be conceived in general. Eternity is not the same as chronological time, merely leaving aside beginning and end in a hypothetical way, or a time empirically read as "Always—Never." As there is an absolute difference between the having-being of God and that of the creature, similarly, eternity and temporality must be understood as ways of being appropriate to God and to the creature, respectively. The absolute self-identity of God with himself, i.e., his being and self-realization, is God's eternity. He does not exist "in" eternity such that his existence only comes about as a result of a fortuitous inclusion into eternity in his own way. There is no eternity apart from God. God's being is his eternity. However, since we do not know God in his essence, through which he is God, we also do not know what eternity is in any fundamental way. We only have an analogous knowledge through his outwardly directed acts through the being in which all beings, by participation in it, have their existence and whose degree of participation in being is determined in their essence.

That every finite existence must first come into its fullness through the realization of its potentials, with which it is not identical, is grounded in the experience of finite being in a manner of consummation which we refer to as time. The realization of man in the sequential order of moments is his temporality and finiteness (as determined by his essence). In death, at the end and conclusion of our freedom narrative, we cannot leave being in time as such behind us. It merely loses the distracting, decaying, unenclosed, fraying and melting quality. The difference between being and essence, between existence and the activity of our capacity—spirit and freedom—remains otherwise we would of necessity become identical with God. Only in God do being and life merge completely into each other. God's self-mediation in Christ, in which he revealed himself for us in his decisiveness, is the foundation of the unlosability of our act of being. Yet we are essentially different from God and not essentially eternal, but rather only eternal *per analogiam et participationem*. But this also grants us a spirit and a will, active agents whose influence reaches out to participate in personal-dialogue in the realization of the life of God, in his self-knowledge in the eternal Word and his self-love in the Holy Spirit, whose divine name, in which he is revealed, is fellowship (2 Cor 13:13) or love (Rom 5:5). It is in this that the saved lives eternally in the co-accomplishment of the trinitarian processions and relations of the God-Eternity.

When people ask about the being of the damned—hypothetically only because we, of course, do not know whether, apart from demons, there will be any—then, first, the positive biblical and ecclesiastical doctrine must be kept in mind that they too will be corporeally resurrected. For corporeity is part of man's essential constitution. They will be kept eternally within the existence of God, without being able to let themselves be fulfilled by his eternal love. Would not destruction be more merciful than eternal damnation? This stands in opposition to the clear biblical and ecclesiastical doctrine of the eternity of the punishments of hell. That is why the threatening biblical words of the destruction of evil are not understood as an annihilation of its being. What is meant is a rendering harmless of their activity directed against God's salvific will that finds its end at the time of their death. Eternal punishment requires the existence of the bearer of this punishment. Would God ever withdrew their being from them, then hell, seen from God's perspective, would be his ad mission of his failed salvific will or a form of self-satisfying revenge. If the damned could only awaken a mere spark of supernatural love for God they would be on the path of penitence and repentance. But that is impossible because death is the end of the freedom history.

But can anyone—speaking exclusively anthropomorphically—imagine God in the midst of his saints, in a communion of blessed love, while below them, in a condition of unremitting hopelessness some men are damned to vegetation? Heaven and hell as the confirmed or rejected acceptance of God's self-mediation in the God–Man Jesus Christ are personal-soteriological relations and their character not similar to the anthropomorphically imagined places of ease or dis-ease. In heaven the saints do not fluctuate between experiencing their own joy and pity for the damned. They see everything in the light of God's righteousness. They conform with his will. They can only rejoice in God and in everything that God is, who is completely the content of their willful orientation, i.e., of their love, from which all joy proceeds, so that grief through an opposite impression must be impossible. Hell, freedom perverted, must remain an impervious "mystery of lawlessness" (2 Thess 2:7).

## b) Theological and Scientific Discussion about the "End of the World"

As is generally accepted, since the beginnings of the modern scientific age, there has been enormous tension to the theological statements regarding the beginning and end of the world which are framed in ideas whose substance reflects a dated image of the world. The empirical understanding of the world in the present is based not only on an extension of the temporal and spatial dimensions of natural and human history into the unimaginable.

The beginning and the end are, factually, metaphysical-anthropologically relations to God. Because the material creation is integrated in man, although it precedes the appearance of man in what is known as natural history in a temporally evolutionary sense, matter is consummated with him and in him in the eternal communion of the corporeal-spiritual being man with God. Of course, inversely, the loss of the communion of the grace of man with God in the beginning of the divine-human dialog also had a negative impact on the whole material and animal world and already encompassed them in temporal anticipation as well.

Hence, we do not obtain the theological reality of the original status or the end status by prolonging our empirically objective image of the world and adding theological statements to it, but rather by transcending them to arrive at the factual statement of the dialogic relationship of man as a spiritual and free creature with his creator, redeemer and consummator, God (cf. 1 Cor 3:22 f.: "World or life or death, or the present or the future: all belong to you, and you to Christ, and Christ to God"). A complete unity of transcendental and categorical possession of reality will only be given to us when we participate in grace in God's eternal knowledge of his self and when we ourselves then also know the world, history and being in his Word, through which he knowingly brings forth the world, and are with him in love.

## c) The Nuptial Unity of the World with God in Jesus Christ

If consummation is only conceivable as an interactive exchange between God and man in a covenant partnership of pure love, then only Christ can be the center and the source of this *sacrum commercium*, of the nuptial communion of the lamb and his bride, the

Church (Rev 19:7), that prayer with the Holy Spirit for the coming of the reign of God at the end of days (Rev 22:17). It is in this way, through Christ, that the world has come to God and become saturated by the divine. Then the kingdom of God appears as the revelation of the glory of the Father. "He has made known to us the mystery of his will...to sum up all things in Christ, in heaven and on earth" (Eph 1:9 f.). In Christ the universal and all-encompassing was able to become concretely tangible, and the individual, that threatens to become lost in the ocean of events and the huge multitudes of men, can become the center of creation in which it is subsumed and goes beyond on its way towards its goal. Hence, we understand Christ as the *universale concretum.* He is the eschatological man, the completely new and eternally young, never changing man, through whom, based on absolute choice, all things are held together, and through whom all things are reconciled, making peace by the blood of his cross (Col 1:19-20), and who was made the first-born from the dead, for in him were created all things in heaven and on earth, the visible and invisible, and who was made the head of the Church and the vital principle of the saints.

With Christ in mind, who was sent by the Father, and the communion which we, in the Holy Spirit (Rev 22:17), have with him, the hymn of thanks of the redeemed creation will grow more and more until the end of the consummation: "The Lord has established his reign, our God, the almighty" (Rev 19:6). In anticipation of the wedding feast with Christ, the faithful call to one another:

> Let us rejoice and be glad and give him glory. For the wedding day of the lamb has come, his bride has made herself ready. (Rev 19:7)

# ABBREVIATIONS

**Magisterial documents quoted are sourced from the following collections:**

DH  Henrici Denzinger, Enchiridion symbolorum definitionum et declarationum de rebus fidei et morum, Latin - English, edited by Peter Hünermann for the original bilingual edition and edited by Robert Fastiggi and Anne Englund Nash for the English edition, Forty-Third Edition, Ignatius Press, San Francisco 2012 (the relevant materials are the Latin or Greek originals)

NR  J. Neuner, H. Roos, Der Glaube der Kirche in den Urkunden der Lehrverkündigung, Rb 121986

**The documents of the Second Vatican Council are quoted as follows:**

Documents of the Second Vatican Council
http://www.vatican.va/archive/hist_councils/ii_vatican_council/index.htm

AA  *Apostolicam Actuositatem*, Decree on the Apostolate of the Laity, November 18, 1965

AG  *Ad Gentes*, Decree on the Mission Activity of the Church, December 7, 1965

CD  *Christus Dominus*, Decree Concerning the Pastoral Office of Bishops in the Church, Oktober 28, 1965

DH  *Dignitatis Humanae*, Declaration on Religious Freedom, December 7, 1965

DV  *Dei Verbum*, Dogmatic Constitution on Divine Revelation, November 18, 1965

GE  *Gravissimum Educationis*, Declaration on Christian Education, October 28, 1965

GS   *Gaudium et Spes*, Pastoral Constitution on the Church in the Modern World, December 7, 1965

IM   *Inter Mirifica*, Decree on Mass Communication Media, December 4, 1963

LG   *Lumen Gentium*, Dogmatic Constitution on the Church, November 21, 1964

NA   *Nostra Aetate*, Declaration on the Relationship of the Church to non-Christian Religions, October 28, 1965

OE   *Orientalium Ecclesiarum*, Decree on the Catholic Churches of the Eastern Rite, November 21, 1964

OT   *Optatam Totius*, Decree on Priestly Training, October 28, 1965

PC   *Perfectae Caritatis*, Decree on the Adaptation and Renewal of the Religious Life, October 28, 1965

PO   *Presbyterorum Ordinis*, Decree on the Ministry and Life of Priests, December 7, 1965

SC   *Sacrosanctum Concilium*, Constitution on the Sacred Liturgy, December 4, 1963

UR   *Unitatis Redintegratio*, Decree on Ecumenism, November 21, 1964

## Abbreviations of the works of classical authors

| Ambrose | in Ps. = | Explanatio XII Psalmorum |
|---|---|---|
| Aristotle | metaph. = | Metaphysica |
| Athenagoras | leg. / suppl. = | Legatio (Supplicatio) pro Christianis |
| | res. = | De resurrectione mortuorum |
| Augustine | civ. = | De civitate dei |
| | conf. = | Confessiones |
| | De cura pro mort. ger. = | De cura pro mortuis gerenda |
| | De Genesi contra Manich. = | De Genesi contra Manichaeos |
| | enchir. = | Enchiridon (Ad Laurentium de fide spe et caritate) |
| | Gen. ad litt. = | De Genesi ad litteram |
| | trin. = | De trinitate |

| | | |
|---|---|---|
| Caesarius of Arles | serm. | Sermones |
| John Calvin | Inst. christ. rel. = | Institutio christianae religionis |
| Clement of Alexandria | protr. = | Protrepticus |
| Cyprian of Carthago | ep. = | Epistulae |
| John Duns Scotus | Op. Ox. (Ord.) Rep. Paris. = | Opus Oxoniense or Ordinatio Reportatio Parisiensis |
| John Scotus Eriugena | De div. nat. = | De divisione naturae |
| Gregory of Nyssa | or. catech. = | Oratio catechetica magna |
| Gregory the Great | dial. = | Dialogi |
| Irenaeus of Lyons | haer. = | Adversus haereses |
| Justin Martyr | 1/2 apol. = dial. = | Apologiae Dialogus cum Tryphone Iudaeo |
| Immanuel Kant | KrV(B) = | Kritik der reinen Vernunft B |
| Lactantius | inst. = | Divinae institutiones |
| Peter Lombard | Sent. = | Libri IV Sententiarum |
| Origen | hom. in = or. = | Homiliae (on the Bible) De oratione |
| Tertullian | an. = monog. = | De anima De monogamia |
| Theophilus of Antioch | Autol. = | Ad Autolycum |
| Thomas Aquinas | S. c. g. = S. th. = | Summa contra gentiles Summa theologiae |
| William of Ockham | Ord. = Quodl. = | Ordinatio (In I Sententiarum) Quodlibeta septem |

## The works of the Apostolic Fathers

| Clement of Rome | 1 Clem. | First Clement |
|---|---|---|
| Ignatius of Antioch | Eph. | Epistula ad Ephesios |
| | Magn. | Epistola ad Magnesios |
| | Philad. | Epistola ad Philadelphienses |
| | Polyc. | Epistola ad Polycarpum |
| | Rom. | Epistola ad Romanos |
| | Mart. Pol. | Martyrium Polycarpi |
| Hermas | mand. | Mandata pastoris |
| | Did. | Didache |
| | Barn. | Letter of Barnabas |

## Place of the publisher

| | | | |
|---|---|---|---|
| B | Berlin | Lo | London |
| D | Düsseldorf | M | München |
| Da | Darmstadt | Ma | Madrid |
| Ei | Einsiedeln | Ms | Münster |
| Ii | Erlangen | Mz | Mainz |
| F | Frankfurt a. M. | NY | New York |
| Fr | Freiburg i. Br. | P | Paris |
| Fri | Fribourg / Schweiz | Pb | Paderborn |
| G | Genf | Rb | Regensburg |
| Gi | Gießen | Ro | Rome |
| Gö | Göttingen | S | Salzburg |
| Gt | Gütersloh | St | Stuttgart |
| HH | Hamburg | Tü | Tübingen |
| I | Innsbruck | Wu | Wuppertal |
| K | Köln | Wü | Würzburg |
| L | Leipzig | Z | Zürich |

# BIBLIOGRAPHY

The following bibliography is a selection of largely monographic literature about these two tractates.

## Doctrine of Creation

Bayer, O., Schöpfung als Anrede, Tü 1986;

Beinert, W., Christus und der Kosmos, Fr 1974;

Böhme, W. (ed.), Evolution und Bewußtsein. Über die Grenzen naturwissenschaftlicher Erkenntnis, Karlsruhe 1987;

——— (ed.), Evolution und Gottesglaube. Ein Lese- und Arbeitsbuch zum Gespräch zwischen Naturwissenschaft und Theologie, Gö 1988;

Bosshard, St.N., Erschafft die Welt sich selbst? Die Selbstorganisation von Natur und Mensch aus naturwissenschaftlicher, philosophischer und theologischer Sicht, Fr 1985;

Bresch, C. (ed.), Kann man Gott aus der Natur erkennen? Fr 1990;

Doll, P., Menschenschöpfung und Weltschöpfung in der alttestamentlichen Weisheit, St 1985;

Dümpelmann, L., Kreation als ontisch-ontologisches Verhältnis. Zur Metaphysik der Schöpfungstheologie des Thomas von Aquin, Fr 1969;

Ganoczy, A., Schöpfungslehre, D 21987;

Hattrup, D., Einstein und der würfelnde Gott, Fr 32001

Hengstenberg, H.-E., Evolution und Schöpfung. Eine Antwort auf den Evolutionismus Teilhard de Chardins, Rb 1963;

Kaiser, Ph. / Peters, D.St. (eds.), Evolutionstheorie und Schöpfungsverständnis, Rb 1984;

Lütgert, W., Schöpfung und Offenbarung, Gi 21984;

May, G., Schöpfung aus dem Nichts, B 1978;

Meier, H. (ed.), Die Herausforderung der Evolutionsbiologie, M 21989;

Metz, J.B., Theologie der Welt, Mz 1968;

Meurers, J., Die Frage nach Gott und die Naturwissenschaft, M 1962;

Moltmann, J., Gott in der Schöpfung. Ökologische Schöpfungslehre,
    M 31987;

Neidhart, W. / Ott, H., Krone der Schöpfung? Humanwissenschaften
    und Theologie, St 1977;

Overhage, P. / Rahner, K., Das Problem der Hominisation, Fr 31965;

Overhage, P., Die biologische Zukunft der Menschheit, F 1977;

Peña, J.L.R. de la, Teología de la creación, Bilbao 21986;

Rahner, H., Der spielende Mensch, Ei 1952;

Saxer, E., Vorsehung und Verheißung Gottes. Vier theologische Mod-
    elle (Calvin, Schleiermacher, Barth, Sölle) und ein systematischer
    Versuch, Z 1980;

Scheffczyk, L., Einführung in die Schöpfungslehre, Da 31987;

Schlier, H., Mächte und Gewalten im Neuen Testament, Fr 31959;

Schmitz-Moormann, K. (ed.), Schöpfung und Evolution, D 1992;

Schneider, Th. / Ullrich, L., Vorsehung und Handeln Gottes, Fr 1988;

Spaemann, R. u.a. (eds.), Evolutionismus und Christentum, Weinheim
    1986;

Thils, G., Theologie der irdischen Wirklichkeiten, S o.J. ((o. J. deutsch:
    ohne Jahr))

Welker, M., Universalität Gottes und Relativität der Welt, Neukirchen
    21988

Westermann, C., Schöpfung, St 1971;

Wilhelm, F., Der Gang der Evolution. Die Geschichte des Kosmos, der
    Erde und des Menschen, M 1987;

Wölfel, E., Welt als Schöpfung. Zu den Fundamentalsätzen der christ-
    lichen Schöpfungslehre heute, M 1981;

## Eschatology

Ahlbrecht, A., Tod und Unsterblichkeit in der evanglischen Theologie
    der Gegenwart. Darlegung und kritische Stellungnahme, Pb 1963;

Althaus, P., Die letzten Dinge, Gt 91964;

Asendorf, U., Eschatologie bei Luther, Gö 1967;

Atzberger, L., Geschichte der christlichen Eschatologie innerhalb der
    vornicänischen Zeit, Fr 1896;

Auer, J., "Siehe, ich mache alles neu." Der Glaube an die Vollendung
    der Welt, Rb 1984;

Bachl, G., Über den Tod und das Leben danach, Graz 1980;

Becker, J., Auferstehung im Urchristentum, St 1976;

Boff, L., Was kommt nach dem Tode? Das Leben nach dem Tode, S
    1982;

Breuning, W. (ed.), Seele. Problembegriff christlicher Eschatologie, Fr
    1986;

Bühlmann, W., Leben - Sterben - Leben. Fragen um Tod und Jenseits,
    Graz 1985;

Dexinger, F. (ed.), Tod - Hoffnung - Jenseits. Dimensionen und Konse-
    quenzen biblisch verankerter Eschatologie, W 1983;

Fasthenrath, E., "In vitam aeternam," Grundzüge christlicher Eschato-
    logie in der ersten Hälfte des 20. Jahrhunderts, St. Ottilien 1982;

Finkenzeller, J., Was kommt nach dem Tod? Eine Orientierungshilfe
    für Unterricht, Verkündigung und Glaubensgespräch, M 21979;

Fischer, J.A., Studien zum Todesgedanken in der alten Kirche. Die
    Beurteilung des natürlichen Todes in der kirchlichen Literatur der
    ersten drei Jahrhunderte, Bd. 1, M 1954;

Fleischbach, E., Fegfeuer. Die christlichen Vorstellungen vom Geschick
    der Verstorbenen, geschichtlich dargestellt, Tü 1969;

Gerhards, A. (ed.), Die größere Hoffnung der Christen, Fr 1990;

Greshake, G. / Kremer, J., Resurrectio mortuorum. Zum theologischen
    Verständnis der leiblichen Auferstehung, Da 1986;

Greshake, G. / Lohfink, G., Naherwartung - Auferstehung - Unsterb-
    lichkeit. Untersuchungen zur christlichen Eschatologie, Fr 41982;

Hattrup, D., Eschatologie, Pb 1992;

Hengstenberg, H.E., Der Leib und die letzten Dinge, Rb 1955;

Jüngel, E., Tod, St 1971;

Kehl, M., Eschatologie, Wü 1986;

Klauck, H.-J. (ed.), Weltgericht und Vollendung, Fr 1994;

Kreck, W., Die Zukunft des Gekommenen. Grundprobleme der
    Eschatologie, M 1961;

Küng, H., Ewiges Leben? M 51985;

Le Goff, J., Die Geburt des Fegfeuers, St 1984;

Libaño, J.B. / Lucchetti Bingemer, M.C., Christliche Eschatologie, D
    1987;

Müller-Goldkuhle, P., Die Eschatologie in der Dogmatik des 19. Jahrhunderts, Essen 1966;

Mußner, F., Was lehrt Jesus über das Ende der Welt? Eine Auslegung von Mk 13, Fr 1958;

Ölsner, W., Die Entwicklung der Eschatologie von Schleiermacher bis zur Gegenwart, Gt 1929 (Ms 1983);

Ott, H., Eschatologie. Versuch eines dogmatischen Grundrisses, Z 1958;

Pieper, J., Tod und Unsterblichkeit, M 21979;

Rahner, K., Zur Theologie des Todes, Fr 1959;

Ratzinger, J. Eschatologie - Tod und ewiges Leben, Rb 1977;

Sauter, G., Zukunft und Verheißung. Das Problem der Zukunft in der gegenwärtigen theologischen und philosophischen Diskussion, Z 1965;

Sonnemans, H., Seele - Unsterblichkeit - Auferstehung. Zur griechischen und christlichen Anthropologie und Eschatologie, Fr 1984;

Scheffczyk, L., Auferstehung. Prinzip christlichen Glaubens, Ei 1976;

Schelkle, K.H., Vollendung von Schöpfung und Erlösung, D 1974;

Scherer, G., Das Problem des Todes in der Philosophie, Da 1979;

Vögtle, A., Das Neue Testament und die Zukunft des Kosmos, D 1970;

Volz, P., Die Eschatologie der jüdischen Gemeinde im neutestamentlichen Zeitalter, Tü 1934;

Vorgrimler, H., Der Tod im Denken und Leben des Christen, D 21982;

——— , Hoffnung auf Vollendung. Aufriß der Eschatologie, Fr 1984;

Waldenfels, H. (ed.), Ein Leben nach dem Leben? Die Antwort der Religionen, D 1988;

Weber, H.J., Die Lehre von der Auferstehung der Toten in den Haupttraktaten der scholastischen Theologie von Alexander von Hales zu Duns Skotus, Fr 1973;

Wiederkehr, D., Perspektiven der Eschatologie, Z 1974;

Wiplinger, F., Der personal verstandene Tod. Todeserfahrung als Selbsterfahrung, Fr 1970;

Wohlgeschaft, A., Hoffnung angesichts des Todes. Das Todesverständnis bei K. Barth und in der zeitgenössischen Theologie des deutschen Sprachraums, Pb 1977;

Woschitz, K.M., Elpis - Hoffnung. Geschichte, Philosophie, Exegese, Theologie eines Schlüsselbegriffs, Fr 1979;